The Demon at Agi Bridge

AND OTHER JAPANESE TALES

TRANSLATIONS FROM THE ASIAN CLASSICS

The Demon at Agi Bridge

AND OTHER JAPANESE TALES

Translated by
BURTON WATSON

Edited, with an introduction, by
HARUO SHIRANE

COLUMBIA UNIVERSITY PRESS   NEW YORK

Columbia University Press wishes to express its appreciation
for assistance given by the Pushkin Fund toward the cost of publishing this book.

Columbia University Press
Publishers Since 1893
New York   Chichester, West Sussex

Library of Congress Cataloging-in-Publication Data
The demon at Agi Bridge and other Japanese tales / translated by Burton Watson ;
edited, with an introduction, by Haruo Shirane.
p. cm. — (Translations from the Asian classics)
Includes bibliographical references.
ISBN 978-0-231-15244-0 (cloth : alk. paper)
ISBN 978-0-231-15245-7 (pbk. : alk. paper)
ISBN 978-0-231-52630-2 (e-book)
1. Folk literature, Japanese. 2. Tales—Japan. 3. Japanese literature—To 1600.
I. Watson, Burton, 1925– II. Shirane, Haruo, 1951–

GR 340.D43   2010
398.20952—dc22   2010018857

Columbia University Press books are printed on permanent and durable acid-free paper.
This book is printed on paper with recycled content.

Printed in the United States of America

c 10 9 8 7 6 5 4 3 2 1
p 10 9 8 7 6

CONTENTS

PREFACE AND ACKNOWLEDGMENTS

The Demon at Agi Bridge and Other Japanese Tales is designed for both the classroom and the general reader who would like to experience the richness of the fascinating and influential body of Japanese anecdotal literature in compact form. I chose the tales in this anthology from the many thousands of stories that appear in *setsuwa* (anecdotal literature) collections for the historical importance and impact of a specific story on the larger tradition of Japanese literary and folk culture, the ability of that story to represent the character and function of a particular *setsuwa* collection, and, most of all, the stories' readability in English and sheer entertainment value.

I would like to acknowledge the aid of my good friend and colleague Komine Kazuaki of Rikkyo University, who helped me with the initial choices of these stories and whose scholarship has been a great inspiration to me. I would like to thank the outside readers of the manuscript, especially David Bialock, who made some key suggestions. I am indebted to David Atherton, who compiled the bibliography and who made very insightful recommendations for the chapter on *Tales of Times Now Past*. My thanks also go to Michiko Tsuneda, who was my research assistant in the final stages of this project. Most of all, I want to thank Burton Watson, the translator, for his patience and diligence over these years.

With the exception of the illustration from the *Konjaku monogatari Picture Scroll* (reprinted by permission of the National Diet Library), all the illustrations for *Tales of Times Now Past*, *A Collection of Tales from Uji*, and *Tales of Renunciation* are from Edo-period wood-block editions of those texts, reprinted with the permission of Komine Kazuaki.

Haruo Shirane

A NOTE ON THE TRANSLATIONS

The translations are from the following sources: Izumoji Osamu, ed., *Nihon ryōiki*, Shin Nihon koten bungaku taikei 30 (Tokyo: Iwanami shoten, 1996); Ikegami Jun'ichi, ed., *Konjaku monogatari shū*, Shin Nihon koten bungaku taikei 33–37 (Tokyo: Iwanami shoten, 1993–1999); Miki Sumito et al., eds., *Uji shūi monogatari*, Shin Nihon koten bungaku taikei 42 (Tokyo: Iwanami shoten, 1990); Nishio Kōichi and Kobayashi Yasuharu, eds., *Kokon chomonjū*, Shinchō Nihon koten shūsei 59, 76 (Tokyo: Shinchōsha, 1983, 1986); Koizumi Hiroshi et al., eds, *Hōbutsushū, Kankyo no tomo, Hirasan kojin reitaku*, Shin Nihon koten bungaku taikei 40 (Tokyo: Iwanami shoten, 1993); Nishio Kōichi, ed., *Senjūshō*, Iwanami bunko 30 (Tokyo: Iwanami shoten, 1970); and Watanabe Tsunaya, ed., *Shasekishū*, Nihon koten bungaku taikei 85 (Tokyo: Iwanami shoten, 1966).

The Demon at Agi Bridge

AND OTHER JAPANESE TALES

INTRODUCTION TO
ANECDOTAL (*SETSUWA*) LITERATURE

Setsuwa (anecdotes), which literally means "spoken story," refers to stories that were first orally narrated and then written down. These recorded stories were often retold, resulting in new variations, which were again recorded. The result is that *setsuwa* frequently exist in multiple variants, with a story usually evolving or serving different purposes over time. In being told, written, retold, and rewritten, these *setsuwa* presume a narrator and a listener, but not necessarily a specific author. *Setsuwa* in this sense began as early as the Nara period (710–784), with the *fudoki* (local gazetteers), which gathered spoken or written stories from the provinces and recorded them in *kanbun* (Chinese-style writing) for the central government. *Setsuwa* as spoken-and-heard narration was stressed by Yanagita Kunio (1875–1962), the founder of *minzokugaku* (folklore studies) in Japan, who sought out "literature before the written word" and who was influential in the modern reevaluation of *setsuwa*. However, premodern *setsuwa* survive only in written form, sometimes in *kanbun* prose, providing a glimpse of the storytelling process but never reproducing it.

Another significant context of *setsuwa* is the *setsuwa-shū* (collection of *setsuwa*), a written genre that had its own structure and conventions, inspired in part by Chinese encyclopedias (*leishu*). In contrast to the first meaning of *setsuwa*, which has its roots in oral storytelling, the *setsuwa-shū* was a literary form that provided a structured worldview and that categorized that world into different spheres and topics. For example, *Tales of Times Now Past* (*Konjaku monogatari shū*, ca. 1120), which contains close to a thousand stories, divides the world into India, China, and Japan, and separates Japan into Buddhist and secular spheres, with the latter being further divided into such secular topics as warriors, poetry, thieves, and humor. The first such *setsuwa* collection is *Record of Miraculous Events in Japan* (*Nihon ryōiki*, ca. 822), a Buddhist anthology that was compiled and edited by Keikai in the early Heian period (794–1185). The *Nihon ryōki* probably functioned as a sermon manual or sermon digest for Buddhist priests who used the stories to appeal to a broad audience. Although we sometimes know the editors of *setsuwa-shū*, such as Priest Mujū (1226–1312), the editor of *Collection of Sand and Pebbles* (*Shasekishū*, 1279–1283), the *setsuwa* themselves are anonymous. In short, there are three key elements to understanding *setsuwa*:

- The act of narration (storytelling)
- The act of writing, which records the spoken story or rewrites an earlier *setsuwa*
- The act of editing, which brings together the stories in a certain order or by topic

In late Heian and medieval aristocratic society, when hereditary family schools were established in fields such as *waka* (classical poetry) and music, the secrets of the family school were passed from teacher to disciple or from the head of the family to his successor by means of *kuden* (secret transmissions). When the line of transmission faced extinction, the family secrets were often written in the form of *setsuwa* in an attempt to preserve the knowledge of the past and of the school. In the late Heian period, this resulted in the *Ōe Conversations* (*Gōdanshō*), a *setsuwa* collection that records the stories narrated by Ōe no Masafusa (1041–1111), one of the leading scholars and poets of the time. In 1111, Ōe no Masafusa, at the age of seventy, fearing that the Ōe lineage would disappear with his death, narrated the family secrets to his top disciple, Fujiwara no Sanekane, who took notes, referred to as *kikigaki* (lecture notes; literally, "listen and write down"). The *Gōdanshō* takes the form of a dialogue between the narrator and the listener. This kind of *setsuwa*, which emerged in the late Heian period, was the product of an age in which knowledge about aristocratic culture and its historical precedents was held in high esteem but was quickly disappearing as the aristocracy fell from power. In this regard,

setsuwa can be considered as a form of topical history, a history that is narrated before it is written.[1]

The systematic attempt to provide knowledge of the past, particularly of
the aristocratic past, is evident in *A Collection of Things Written and Heard
in the Past and Present* (*Kokon chomonjū*, ca. 1254), which was edited by
Tachibana Narisue, a low-ranking aristocrat and literatus who received the
secret transmission on a biwa (lute). In the preface, Narisue asserts that
Kokon chomonjū begins where *A Collection of Tales from Uji* (*Uji shūi monogatari*, early thirteenth century), the most popular of the *setsuwa* collections in the premodern period, leaves off and is intended to augment the
official histories. The collection, whose structure shows the influence of
Chinese encyclopedias, covers a variety of topics, beginning with Shinto,
Buddhism, government, court matters, Chinese literature, classical poetry,
and calligraphy, and ending with plants and trees (section 29) and fish,
insects, and animals (section 30).

In contrast to the narrational setting of the *Gōdanshō*, which was based
on a vertical teacher–disciple relationship, other *setsuwa* were born out of
an open relationship among people from different backgrounds—from
commoners to samurai to aristocrats—who gathered to tell or hear stories.
This was probably the setting that resulted in the *setsuwa* "How the Demon
at Agi Bridge in Ōmi Province Ate Somebody" (27:13), which appears
in book 27 of the *Konjaku monogatari shū*. These kinds of stories about
demons probably had no particular value for a family or profession, but
they were of great interest to those who heard them, and book 27, which
is devoted to *oni* (demon) stories, provides a systematic glimpse into this
aspect of the world.

Storytelling in the Heian and medieval periods took various forms.
One type was the "round-table" format, referred to as *meguri-monogatari*
or *jun-no-monogatari* (tales in order), in which participants took turns telling stories, often with a listener who was an aristocrat and could write. In
the preface to the *Uji shūi monogatari*, the Senior Counselor (*Dainagon*)
of Uji, Minamoto no Takakuni (1004–1077), resting near the Byōdō-in

---

1. Komine Kazuaki, "Setsuwa no katachi o tsukamu," in *Chūsei no sekai o yomu*, Iwanami
seminaabukkusu 69 (Tokyo: Iwanami shoten, 1998), 27–29.

Temple at Uji, south of the capital (present-day Kyoto), calls out to passers-by and has them tell their stories, which he writes down. The *Uji shūi monogatari* can be said to derive from Takakuni's *kikigaki* on what he heard by the roadside. This format even pervades the court literature of the Heian period. *The Great Mirror* (*Ōkagami*, late eleventh century), a history written in vernacular Japanese that describes the age of the Fujiwara regents, who controlled the throne and political power in the tenth and eleventh centuries, and the rise of Fujiwara no Michinaga (966–1027), similarly begins on a rainy evening when nobles gather before the retired emperor Kazan (r. 984–986) to tell their stories. Frequently, the storytellers met in the evening and told stories into the morning, in a pattern called *tsuya-monogatari* (all-night tales). This custom of round-table or all-night storytelling continued into the Edo (Tokugawa) period (1600–1867) and resulted in such customs as the *hyaku monogatari* (hundred tales), in which each participant told a ghost story and, when all had finished, the candle was blown out, allowing a "real" ghost to appear.

In the famous conversations about women on a rainy night (*amayo no shinasadame*) in the "Broomtree" (Hahakigi) chapter of *The Tale of Genji* (*Genji monogatari*, early eleventh century), Tō no Chūjō, Genji, and their male friends take turns telling stories about women whom they have known. As the example of *Genji* suggests, oral storytelling and story listening not only was the source of *setsuwa*, but was incorporated into Heian *monogatari* (court tales). Indeed, one of the major characteristics of Heian and early medieval court tales is the presence of a narrator or narrators through whom the action is viewed and the character's words are heard. Often taking the form of female attendants, the narrators reside within the world of the characters.

Since one of the objectives of such *setsuwa* collections as the *Konjaku monogatari shū* of the late Heian period and *Transmissions from Three Countries* (*Sangoku denki*, early fifteenth century), edited by Gentō, was to provide an encyclopedic worldview—centered on India, China, and Japan—they gathered stories from these countries. *Tales of China* (*Kara monogatari*, ca. 1165), perhaps edited by Fujiwara no Shigenori (1135–1188), is a collection of adaptations, in the style of *uta-monogatari* (poem-tales), from Chinese texts such as *Records of the Historian* (*Shiji*, Jp. *Shiki*), *Book of*

Han (*Hanshu*, Jp. *Hansho*), *Meng qiu* (Jp. *Mōgyū*),[2] and *Collected Works of Bo Juyi* (*Boshi wenji*, Jp. *Hakushi monjū*). In *Sangoku denki*, from the Muromachi period (1392–1573), a Buddhist priest from India, a layperson from China, and a person from Japan tell stories about their respective countries. The Chinese had already translated parts of Buddhist scriptures and stories from Sanskrit into Chinese, and they were then transmitted to Japan. These translations from the Chinese were, in turn, orally narrated and written down again. The tales from India and China in the *Konjaku monogatari shū* had been circulated and narrated before being recorded and often differ significantly from their Chinese sources. Given the nature of *setsuwa*, which were not concerned with the notion of an authentic original text, these *setsuwa* are best regarded as free adaptations. Japanese knowledge of Chinese historical figures and legends as they appear in medieval *gunkimono* (warrior tales), such as *The Tales of the Heike* (*Heike monogatari*, from mid-thirteenth century onward), was often derived from such *setsuwa* rather than from the original Chinese text or Confucian classic.

The language and style of the *setsuwa* are diverse. The first *setsuwa* collection, the *Nihon ryōiki*, was written in *hentai kanbun* (literally, "unorthodox Chinese"). The *Konjaku monogatari shū* was written in *wakan-konkōbun*, a compact and highly efficient Sino-Japanese style that mixes Chinese graphs with *katakana*, a Japanese syllabary associated with Buddhist writing. The *Uji shūi monogatari* uses *hiragana*, in a more classical style that draws on the court tale tradition. The *Sangoku denki* is written in *kanbun* (Chinese-style writing). These texts, which reveal a wide range of written styles, cannot be said to be direct recordings of oral performances.

In the Heian period, *setsuwa* were regarded by Buddhist priests as a means to spread Buddhism and make it accessible to an audience that could not read Buddhist scriptures. This partially accounts for the large number of Buddhist-centered *setsuwa* collections in the late Heian and early Kamakura (1183–1333) periods. The editors, such as those of the *Konjaku monogatari shū*, were interested in China and India not only because they wanted to present a world history but because Buddhism had spread

---

2. Li Han and Hsu Tzu-kuang, *Meng Ch'iu: Famous Episodes from Chinese History and Legend*, trans. Burton Watson (Tokyo: Kodansha International, 1979).

from India through China to Japan. With the rise of Zen Buddhism in the Kamakura period and the emergence of Buddhist leaders such as Eisai (1141–1215), the Rinzai Zen leader, and Dōgen (1200–1253), the Sōtō Zen pioneer, who stressed enlightenment without words and beyond language, the Buddhist attitude toward *setsuwa* as a component of religious education changed, and *setsuwa* were sometimes banned as a tool for teaching.[3]

The *setsuwa* collections embrace a wide variety of topics—from poetry to violence to sex to humor—and their contents range from folktales about animals and plants to historical legends to myths about gods to accounts about everyday commoner life to stories of the supernatural. If there is a common denominator in this huge variety, it was the attempt by the editors to provide a comprehensive vision of the world and a means to survive in the world. The readers/listeners were expected to learn a "lesson" about some aspect of life. This is apparent in the predilection for didactic endings. The editor or writer/recorder gave each *setsuwa* a particular function. The same story may appear in one collection as a Buddhist *setsuwa* and in another collection as a secular *setsuwa*. The didactic endings are particularly prominent in the Buddhist collections, which were attempting to spread the Buddhist gospel or to stress the efficacy of the Lotus Sutra or the power of the bodhisattva Kannon (Avalokiteśvara). The *setsuwa* often end with what are now called *kotowaza*, or aphorisms that provide guidance in navigating life. For example, "On Receiving the Immediate Penalty of an Evil Death for Collecting Debts in an Unreasonable Manner and with High Interest" (*Nihon ryōiki*, 3:26) concludes with the phrase "Those who fail to repay debts that they owe will atone for this by becoming a horse or an ox." An example of a modern aphorism is *akuin akka* (bad cause, bad results), which means something like "you reap what you sow" and which derives from the Buddhist notion of karmic retribution. The use of stories that have been heard or circulated for pedagogical purposes also was common in medieval *zuihitsu* (free-form essays), such as Priest Kenkō's *Essays in Idleness* (*Tsurezuregusa*, 1329–1333), some of which closely resemble *setsuwa* collections.

---

3. Komine, "Setsuwa no katachi o tsukamu," 15–16.

Another major characteristic of *setsuwa* was that they were not confined to the world of the court and the aristocracy in the way that Heian court tales and classical poetry tended to be. Instead, *setsuwa* embraced a wide range of social groups, encompassing commoners, warriors, priests, and aristocrats. The *Konjaku monogatari shū*, compiled in the twelfth century, is one of the first collections that includes stories about warriors, who were emerging as a social class in the Heian period. These anthologies also explore the underworld of thieves, pirates, and social deviants. When compared with the early chronicles, such as the *Chronicles of Japan* (*Nihon shoki*, 720), or the late Heian, Kamakura, and Nanboku-chō (1336–1392) vernacular histories, such as the *Ōkagami* and *The Clear Mirror* (*Masuka-gami*, 1338–1376)—which focus on the imperial line, the Fujiwara regency, or retired emperors—the *setsuwa* collections offer a broad view of the underside of history.

The *setsuwa* collections also deal with the divine (gods), the supernatu-ral (ghosts, demons, long-nosed *tengu*, and other otherworldly beings), and the world of dreams, which were thought to provide access to the other world, to those not immediately or physically accessible such as the spirits of the dead and gods. Significantly, the storytelling scenes in *set-suwa* are often set near or at a temple or shrine, where the narrators have implicitly close access to divine spirits. In a related fashion, the stories also provide access to the underworld of the erotic and sexual, which often manifested itself in the form of dreams, spirits, and the supernatural. In the *Konjaku monogatari shū*, for example, snakes, which appear in the earlier *Nihon shoki* as gods (such as the god of Mount Miwa), appear as evil ser-pents and often as phallic symbols. However, in contrast to Heian-period *monogatari*, such as *The Tale of Genji*, which admit to their fictionality, *set-suwa* present the narration as history, as a record of past events, even when these events are about the strange or the miraculous. In the medieval and Edo periods, *setsuwa* collections were generally considered to be a kind of historical record or a type of vernacular Buddhist writing (*hōgo*).

In terms of form, the *setsuwa* differ from court tales and military chron-icles in their brevity, rarely extending beyond five or six pages. They tend to be action-oriented, plot-centered, externally descriptive, and com-pact, often focusing on a single event or a limited chain of events. The collections, by contrast, can be very large—such as the *Konjaku monogatari shū*, with over a thousand tales—have complex thematic structures, and attempt to be comprehensive and historical in coverage. Like the poems in a poetry anthology, the individual *setsuwa* thus can be read both independently and as part of a subgroup of a book (*maki*) or section, in which each story is a variation on a theme such as Kannon, humor, or demons. Within each book, furthermore, successive tales are often linked by a shared topic or motif.

In the late medieval period, the *setsuwa* genre came to be overshadowed by a new genre, the *otogi-zōshi* (Muromachi tale), a longer narrative form that incorporates elements of the Heian court tale and draws on many of the same sources as the *setsuwa* collections. The *setsuwa* collections, however, saw new life in the Edo period when they were printed for the first time, widely read, and compiled anew. Throughout their history, *setsuwa* have provided a constant and deep source of material for other genres, such as the *nikki* (literary diary), *monogatari*, *gunki-mono*, historical chronicles, *nō* drama, *kowakamai* (ballad drama), *kyōgen* (comic theater), *otogi-zōshi*, and *sekkyō-bushi* (sermon ballads). A closely related genre is the warrior tale (such as *Heike monogatari*), which often integrates various shorter *setsuwa* into a longer chronological narrative that traces the arc of a particular war.

In contrast to Heian classical poetry and court tales, which were canonized in the form of the *Kokinshū* (*Collection of Ancient and Modern Poems*, ca. 905), *The Tales of Ise* (*Ise monogatari*, tenth century), and *The Tale of Genji* in the late Heian period, the *setsuwa* collections were not considered serious literature for most of the premodern period and were not the object of commentary or used in school textbooks. The *Uji shūi monogatari* became popular in the Edo period, but the *Konjaku monogatari shū* appears to have been totally neglected until the modern period. It was not until the twentieth century when the *setsuwa* collections drew the attention of modern novelists such as Akutagawa Ryūnosuke (1892–1927)—who adopted and combined the *setsuwa* in such noted modern short stories as "Nose" (Hana) and "Rashōmon"—that *setsuwa* collections such as the *Konjaku monogatari shū* became part of the Japanese literary canon and were referred to as *setsuwa bungaku* (anecdotal literature). Because of their interest in commoner life, the *Uji shūi monogatari* and *Konjaku monogatari shū* became particularly popular after World War II, when Japanese literature was "democratized" and curricular attention was shifted away from military and aristocratic literature.

Keikai (Kyōkai, late eighth to early ninth century), the compiler of *Record of Miraculous Events in Japan* (*Nihon ryōiki*, ca. 822), was a *shidosō* (private priest), as opposed to a publicly recognized and certified priest ordained by the eighth century *ritsuryō* (literally, "law code") state system. (The *ritsuryō* state attempted to keep a tight control on the priesthood and cracked down on private priests, who took vows without official permission, often as a way to avoid taxation and service.) Keikai's accounts of himself in the *Nihon ryōiki* state that in 787 he realized that his current poverty and secular life were the result of evil deeds that he had committed in a previous life and so he decided to become a priest.

In Keikai's time, during the reigns of Emperor Kanmu (r. 781–806) and his son Emperor Saga (r. 809–823), the country was rocked by considerable social disorder, famine, and plagues. It was a particularly hard time for the farmers, many of whom fled from their home villages. Some of these refugees were absorbed into local temples and private estates, and others became private priests. Unlike the official priests in the capital, who had aristocratic origins, the private priests attracted a more plebian constituency, and the *Nihon ryōiki* functioned for them as a kind of handbook of sermons. In this regard, the *Nihon ryōiki* differs significantly from the elite literature being produced at this time, such as *Nostalgic Recollections of Literature* (*Kaifūsō*, 751) and *Collection of Literary Masterpieces* (*Bunka shūreishū*, 818), two noted collections of Chinese poetry and refined Chinese prose written by aristocrats. Instead, the stories in the *Nihon ryōiki* were written in *hentai kanbun*, an unorthodox Chinese-style prose, and depict the underside of society and the reality of everyday commoner life.

The *Nihon ryōiki*, sometimes considered to be Japan's first *setsuwa* (anecdote) collection, bears the signs of earlier oral storytelling. Although 80 percent of the stories take place in the Yamato area, the place-names come from almost every part of the country—from Michinoku (northeastern Honshū) to Higo (in Kyushu)—strongly suggesting that the private priest would preach in a certain village, gather stories, and then tell them in another village, as a storyteller would. In the process, local folk stories and anecdotes became Buddhist parables. Whereas the early chronicles, the *Record of Ancient Matters* (*Kojiki*, 712) and *Chronicles of Japan* (*Nihon shoki*, 720), combined many local and provincial myths and legends into a larger state mythology, the *Nihon ryōiki* absorbed local folk stories and converted them into Buddhist anecdotes. As a consequence, the interest of a number of the stories in the *Nihon ryōiki* is not so much in the Buddhist message as in the story itself, which often is erotic or violent.

As he notes in the introduction, Keikai arranged these stories in such a way as to demonstrate the Buddhist principle of karmic causality, in which the rewards and retributions for past actions are directly manifested in this world. This principle is embodied in the full title of the collection, *Record of Miraculous Cases of Manifest Rewards and Retribution for Good and Evil in Japan* (*Nihonkoku genpō zen'aku ryōi-ki*). The stories generally are one of two types: those in which good deeds are rewarded and those in which evil deeds are punished. Other stories demonstrate the miraculous powers of Buddha, the bodhisattvas, sutras, and Buddhist icons.

In the *Kojiki* and *Nihon shoki*, the underworld (Yomi) is a place marked by pollution where bodies decompose. In the *Nihon ryōiki*, by contrast, we suddenly are confronted with a terrifying Buddhist hell where past actions are severely punished. In the ancient period, sin was often the result of transgressing the communal order, usually agricultural violations or pollutions. But in the *Nihon ryōiki*, sin takes on new meaning as a moral and social violation, with the individual responsible for his or her own actions. In the early chronicles, disease is cured by communal means, by purification and cleansing. But later, disease, which figures prominently in the *Nihon ryōiki*, became the punishment for sin, the result of karmic retribution.

The *Nihon ryōiki* contains 116 stories and is divided into three volumes, which appear to be arranged in chronological order. The effort to present the history of Buddhism is clear, with the climax coming in the Tenpyō era (729–749), during the reign of Emperor Shōmu (r. 724–749), who built the statue of the Great Buddha in the Tōdai-ji temple in Nara and took holy vows. Emperor Shōmu and Priest Gyōki (668–749) figure prominently in volume 2, which represents Buddhism at its apex. Gyōki, who traveled through the countryside teaching Buddhism to commoners in easily understood terms, is perhaps the single most important figure in the *Nihon ryōiki* and reflects Keikai's own position as a private priest. For example, in the story "On Ransoming Some Crabs and a Frog and Setting Them Free, She Was Immediately Rewarded by Being Saved by the Crabs" (2:12), which occurs during Shōmu's reign, Gyōki appears and advises a woman to have faith in the Three Treasures (Buddha, Buddhist law, and the Buddhist priesthood).

Volume 3, by contrast, is strongly pervaded by the notion of *mappō* (the last days of the Buddhist law), which is the last of the three ages of the Buddhist law, an age of decline in which Buddhist teachings are abandoned. As the introduction to the *Nihon ryōiki* contends, Keikai was convinced that the world was in a state of serious decline, if not apocalyptic collapse, and that the sermons based on the *Nihon ryōiki* were necessary to save people from their great sins. In contrast to the later *monogatari* (court tales), which admit to being fiction, the *Nihon ryōiki*, like other *setsuwa* collections, insists on the truth of the stories it offers. That is, to teach the truth of the Buddha, the stories had to be miraculous, but they also had to be presented as truthful.

The story "On a Boy of Great Strength Who Was Born of the Thunder's Rejoicing" (1:3) probably began as a local legend or series of legends from Owari Province that the Gangō-ji temple turned into a Buddhist tale. The *setsuwa* appears to link together a number of disparate stories—the capture of lightning, the gift of a small child who has great strength, a contest of rock-throwing strength, the exorcism of a demon who turns out to be the vengeful spirit of a dead person, and a water contest—that appear in other folktales and legends.

"On the Evil Death Visited Immediately on an Evil and Perverse Son Who, Out of Love for His Wife, Plotted to Kill His Mother" (2:3) revolves around the sin of killing a parent, one of the eight crimes under *ritsuryō* state codes. In Buddhism, it was considered one of the five heinous sins, for which the murderer would go to hell. Similar stories appear in *Tales of Times Now Past* (*Konjaku monogatari shū*, 20:33) and in book 7 of *Collection of Treasures of the Buddhist Law* (*Hōbutsu-shū*, ca. thirteenth century).

The story "On Ransoming Some Crabs" (2:12) appears in similar form in *Record of Miraculous Powers of the Lotus Sutra* (*Hokke genki*, ca. 1040–1044), but without Gyōki's name, at a different place (Kuse), and with a concluding reference to the Kanimata-dera (Crab Temple), indicating that it was an *engi* (story) about the origins of a temple. Similar stories are also found in the *Konjaku monogatari shū* (16:16), *A Collection of Things Written and Heard in Past and Present* (*Kokon chomonjū*, 20:682), and *Collection of Sand and Pebbles* (*Shasekishū*, 8:4).

The story "On Receiving the Immediate Penalty of an Evil Death for Collecting Debts in an Unreasonable Manner and with High Interest" (3:26) is similar to several other *setsuwa* in the *Nihon ryōiki* (such as 1:10) in which a person steals from others and subsequently turns into a cow to be used for labor. This story, however, differs in that the sinner becomes an ox in this life, making the karmic retribution even more dramatic.

※

On a Boy of Great Strength Who Was Born of the Thunder's Rejoicing (1:3)

Long ago in the time of Emperor Bidatsu (who was named Nunakura-futotama-shiki no mikoto and resided in the Palace of Osada in Iware), there was a farmer living in the village of Katawa in the district of Ayu-chi in Owari Province. He was preparing his rice fields and flooding them with water when a light rain began to fall. Accordingly, he took shelter under a tree and stood there holding a metal rod.[1] Presently, it began to thunder. Frightened, the man held the rod over his head, whereupon the thunder dropped down in front of him, taking the form of a young boy who bowed politely.

1. The metal rod presumably is some kind of farm implement.

The man was about to strike him with the rod, but the thunder said, "Please don't harm me! I will repay you for your kindness!"

"How will you repay me?" the man asked.

"I will repay you by seeing that a son is born to you," the thunder replied. "So you must make me a boat of camphor wood, fill it with water, and float bamboo leaves in it."

When the man had done as the thunder had asked, the thunder said, "Don't come any closer!" and withdrew to a great distance, rising to the sky in a cloud of mist. Later, a child was born who had a snake twined twice around his neck, born with the head and tail of the snake hanging down behind.

When the boy had grown to be ten years and more, reports spread of a man at the imperial court who was very strong. Thinking that he would like to try to challenge him, the boy made his way to the emperor's palace. At this time, there was a prince of the royal family who excelled in strength and was living in separate quarters by the northeastern corner of the imperial palace. At the northeastern corner of his quarters was a stone that measured eight feet around. The strong-man prince came out of his quarters, picked up the stone, and threw it some distance. Then he returned to his quarters, shut the gate, and did not admit anyone.

The boy, observing this, thought to himself, "This must be the strong man I've heard about!" That night, when no one was looking, he picked up the stone and threw it one foot farther than the prince had done. The prince, seeing this, rubbed his hands together, picked up the stone, and threw it, but he was unable to throw it any farther than before. The boy then threw the stone two feet farther than the prince's throw. The prince, seeing this and hoping for greater success, threw it again, but did no better than before. When the boy picked up the stone and threw it again, his heels dug three inches into the ground and the stone went three feet farther. The prince, seeing the marks where the boy had stood, thought, "This must be where the boy is!" and ran after him, but the boy ducked through the hedge and fled. The prince leaped over the hedge in pursuit, but the boy turned and fled back to the other side of the hedge. The prince was never able to catch him, and realizing that the boy surpassed him in strength, he gave up the chase.

Later the boy became an apprentice at Gangō-ji temple.[2] At this time, the boys who rang the bell in the bell tower were being killed night after night. The boy, learning of this, said to the monks, "I will catch the ogre, kill him, and put a stop to this plague of death!"

When the monks agreed to this, he had four men stationed with lamps at the four corners of the bell tower and told them, "When I seize the ogre, remove the shades from your lamps!" Then he took his stand by the door of the bell tower.

In the middle of the night, a huge ogre appeared but, spying the boy, withdrew. Later in the night, it came again. The boy seized hold of the ogre's hair and began to pull; the ogre pulled to get away, but the boy pulled toward the inside of the bell tower. The four men who had been stationed in the tower were so terrified that they could not lift the shades from the lamps. The boy then pulled the ogre to each of the four corners of the tower and thus was able to uncover the lamps. When dawn came, it was found that the boy had pulled the ogre's hair out by the roots and the ogre had fled. The next day, they followed the trail of the ogre's blood to see where it would lead. It led to a crossroads where a wicked servant of the temple had been buried. Thus they knew that the ogre was the ghost of the wicked servant.[3] The hair from the ogre's head is preserved to this day in Gangō-ji and is looked on as a treasure of the temple.

The boy later became an *upāsaka*, or lay believer, and continued to live at Gangō-ji. The temple was preparing its rice fields and getting ready to flood them with water. But some princes of the royal family cut off the water supply to the fields, so they became parched. The *upāsaka* said, "I'll see that the water gets into these fields," and the monks agreed to leave things to him.

The *upāsaka* then had a plow handle made so large that it required more then ten men to carry it. Then he picked it up like a staff, carried it to the sluice gate, and stuck it there. But the princes pulled out the plow handle

2. Located at this time in Asuka, Gangō-ji later moved to Nara and became one of the seven great temples of Nara.
3. Persons who had died unfortunate deaths were buried in a roadway, so the feet of people traveling the road could prevent the spirits of the deceased from moving around and causing harm.

and threw it away, so the sluice gate was once more blocked and no water flowed into the temple fields. The *upāsaka* then brought a stone so big that it would take more than a hundred men to carry it and propped the sluice gate open, allowing the water to flow into the temple fields. The princes, awed by his strength, no longer attempted to stop him, and as a result the temple fields did not dry up but produced an excellent crop.

Because of this, the monks agreed to let the *upāsaka* become an ordained monk with the name Dharma Master Dōjō. When people of later times tell of Dharma Master Dōjō of Gangō-ji and his many feats of strength, this is who they mean, and it is right that they should speak so. No doubt he had performed many good and powerful acts of karma in his previous lives and thus was able to acquire this kind of strength. This was a wonderful event that occurred in the land of Japan.

On the Evil Death Visited Immediately on an Evil and Perverse Son Who, Out of Love for His Wife, Plotted to Kill His Mother (2:3)

Kishi no Homaro was from the village of Kamo in the district of Tama in Musashi Province. Homaro's mother was Kusakabe no Matoji. Homaro was appointed by Ōtomo (exact name unknown) to serve for three years as a frontier guard in Tsukushi.[4] His mother accompanied him to see to his needs, while his wife remained in Musashi to look after the house.

At that time, Homaro, separated from his wife, was filled with unbearable longing for her and hit on a perverse scheme, thinking, "If I murder my mother, I will be obliged to tend to her funeral and will be excused from duty and can go home. Then I can be with my wife!"

His mother by nature thought only of doing good deeds, and so the son said to her, "In the hills east of here there is to be a meeting devoted

---

4. In Kyūshū, Tsukushi was where forces were stationed to guard against possible attacks from China or Korea.

to seven days of lectures on the Lotus Sutra. Why don't you go listen to them?" Deceived by these words, the mother set her mind on listening to the sutra. Having bathed in hot water and purified herself, she set off for the mountains in company with her son.

The son, glaring at his mother with ox-like eyes, said to her, "Kneel down on the ground!" Gazing at her son's face, the mother said, "Why do you speak to me like that? Has some demon taken possession of you?" But the son unsheathed a long sword and prepared to cut off his mother's head.

Kneeling before her son, the mother said, "We plant trees in hopes of gathering the fruit and resting in the shade they give. And we raise children in hopes of gaining their help and in time being taken care of by them. But now the tree I have counted on lets the rain leak through! Why has my child turned from his usual thoughts and now wants to do me harm?"

The son, however, paid no heed to her. Then the mother, giving up all hope, took off the clothes she was wearing and put them in three piles. Kneeling before her son, she made this dying request: "Wrap these up as a memento of me. One pile of clothes goes to you, my eldest son. One pile please give to my second son, and one pile to my youngest son."

But when the perverse son stepped forward, preparing to cut off his mother's head, the ground opened and he fell into it. The mother leaped up, ran forward, and seized hold of her son's hair as he fell. Looking up at the heavens, she cried out this plea: "My son is a victim of possession. He does not really mean to do this! Please pardon his offense!" But though she clung to his hair, struggling to save him, in the end he sank into the ground.

The loving mother returned home with the son's hair. Holding a Buddhist service in his memory, she put the hair in a box and placed it before an image of the Buddha, reverently requesting monks to recite scriptures before it.

Because the mother felt profound compassion, she was moved to take pity on her evil and perverse son and to do good on his behalf. Truly one should understand that sins of unfilial conduct meet with immediate requital and that evil and perverse offenses never go unpunished.

On Ransoming Some Crabs and a Frog and Setting Them Free, She Was Immediately Rewarded by Being Saved by the Crabs (2:12)

In Yamashiro Province, in a community in the district of Kii, there was a young woman whose family and personal name are unknown. Tender-hearted by nature, she believed firmly in the law of karma, observed the five precepts and the ten good deeds, and never deprived any living thing of life.[5] In the reign of Emperor Shōmu [r. 724–749], some of the cowherds in the village where she lived caught eight crabs in a mountain stream and were about to roast and eat them. The young woman, seeing this, pleaded with the herd boys, saying, "Please be so kind as to give me the crabs!" But the boys refused to heed her, replying, "We're going to roast them and eat them!" Earnestly she begged and entreated, taking off her cloak and offering it in payment, and finally the boys handed over the crabs to her. She then requested the Meditation Master Gi to perform prayers asking for merit and set the crabs free.

Sometime later, the young woman went into the mountains and came upon a huge snake about to swallow a large frog. She said to the snake imploringly, "If you will only give me that frog, I will present you with numerous offerings of woven goods!" When the snake ignored her and refused to listen, she promised to gather even more woven goods and pray to the snake, saying, "I will worship you like a god if you will heed my pleas and release the frog!" The snake paid no attention, however, and went on

5. The law of karma states that those who create good karma—that is, perform good acts of body, mouth, and mind—will in future existences enjoy favorable circumstances. Conversely, those who do evil will fare badly in future existences. The five precepts for lay believers are prohibitions against killing, stealing, engaging in sexual misconduct, lying, and drinking alcoholic beverages. The ten good deeds are the observance of these five precepts plus that of the precepts against slandering believers, praising oneself and disparaging others, succumbing to greed, expressing anger, and speaking ill of Buddhism.

swallowing the frog. Then she said to the snake, "If you will give me the frog, I will agree to be your wife, so please let it go!" With this, the snake at last took notice of her, lifting up its head, stretching out its neck, and peering into the young woman's face. Then it spat out the frog and let it go. The woman thereupon arranged an assignation with the snake, saying, "Come to me when seven days have passed."

Later, she told her father and mother all about the incident with the snake. They were distraught and said, "You are our only child! How could you have been so insane as to make impossible promises like that?"

At this time, the Eminent Monk Gyōki[6] was in residence at Jinchō-ji temple in the district of Kii, and so the woman went and reported to him what had happened. When he had listened to her, he said, "Ah, what an astounding story! The only thing to do is to have faith in the Three Treasures."

Having received his instructions, she returned home, and when the night for the assignation arrived, she shut the house up tight and prepared to defend herself, making various religious vows and placing her trust in the Three Treasures. The snake circled the house, slithering this way and that on its belly and pounding against the wall with its tail. Then it climbed onto the roof, chewed a hole through the thatch, and dropped down in front of the young woman. But before it could approach her, there was a sudden outburst of noise, with sounds of scrambling, biting, and chewing. The next morning when the young woman looked to see what had happened, she found eight large crabs gathered there, and a snake that had been hacked and slashed into pieces.

If even such lowly and unenlightened creatures know how to repay a debt of gratitude when they have incurred it, how can it be right for human beings to forget the debts they owe? From this time on in Yamashiro Province, great honor was paid to the large crabs that live in the mountain streams, and it was considered an act of goodness to set them free.

---

6. Gyōki (668–749) was a Buddhist priest who was renowned for founding temples, preaching, and devoting himself to bettering the lot of the people.

On Receiving the Immediate Penalty of an Evil Death for Collecting Debts in an Unreasonable Manner and with High Interest (3:26)

Tanaka no mahito Hiromushime was the wife of Oya no agatanushi Miyate of Outer Junior Sixth Rank, Upper Grade, the chief of the district of Miki in Sanuki Province. She gave birth to eight children. She was very rich, possessing many valuables, horses and cattle, male and female slaves, stores of rice and cash, and paddies and dry fields. But by nature she had no sense of rightness; mean and greedy, she never gave anything away. In the case of rice wine, she added lots of water so she could make a greater profit selling it. Days when she was lending, she used a little measuring cup, but a big cup on days when she was collecting debts. She used a small scale in dispensing goods but a large one in exacting repayment. She was utterly unreasonable in matters of interest, sometimes charging ten times the original loan, sometimes a hundred times. She turned a deaf ear to debtors and showed no pity in her heart. As a result, many people, over-come by worries, abandoned their homes and fled to other provinces. No one could match the meanness of her ways.

In the seventh year of the Hōki era [776], the first day of the Sixth Month, Hiromushime, stricken with illness, took to her bed. A number of days passed, and then, on the twentieth day of the Seventh Month, she called her husband and her eight sons to her side and told them what had been revealed to her in dreams.

"I was summoned to the palace of King Yama and shown these dreams. The first represented the crime of making use of many things belonging to the Three Treasures of Buddhism and offering nothing in return. The second represented the crime of adding a lot of water to the wine in order to make a greater profit. The third represented the practice of using two sets of measuring cups and scales, handing out seven-tenths the proper amount when lending but demanding twelve-tenths when receiving repay-ment. 'You have been summoned here because of these three crimes,' said the king. 'You will receive immediate punishment, as I will now show you!'" Having described what the dreams had told her, she died the very same day.

The family delayed her cremation for seven days, meanwhile inviting meditation masters and lay Buddhist believers, thirty-two persons in all, to come together and, for the next nine days, to pray for her good fortune.

On the evening of the seventh day, she came back to life, the lid of her coffin opening of its own accord. Peering into the coffin, the observers were confronted by an unbearable stench. From the waist up, she had already turned into an ox, with horns four inches long growing out of her forehead. Her arms had become the forefeet of an ox; the nails on her hands had split and turned into an ox's hooves. From the waist down, she remained in human form. She had no use for rice but fed on grass, and after she had eaten she chewed her cud. She was naked and without clothes and lay in her filth.

People came running from east and west, gathering around in endless numbers to gaze in wonder at her. Her husband, the chief of the district, and his children, filled with shame and pity, flung themselves to the ground, uttering countless pleas for mercy. To atone for her offenses, they presented various valuable articles from their home as offerings to Miki-ji temple. They also presented seventy cattle, thirty horses, twenty acres of cultivated fields, and four thousand bundles of rice to Tōdai-ji temple, and canceled all debts owed to her. The provincial and district officials were preparing to send a report on her to the authorities when, after five days, she finally died. From all the people of the province and district who had seen her or heard of her came sighs of pity and mourning.

She was blind to the law of cause and effect, unreasonable and lacking in rightness. So we know for certain that unreasonable action invites immediate punishment and lack of rightness calls forth evil results. That she received immediate punishment is only to be expected, to say nothing of penalties to be suffered in her next existence.

As the sutra says, "Those who fail to repay debts that they owe will atone for this by becoming a horse or an ox."[7] The borrower is like a slave;

7. This appears to be a condensation of a passage from the *Treatise on the Establishment of Truth* (Ch. *Chengshilun*, Jp. *Jōjitsuron*, 412), a Chinese translation of an Indian work (*Satyasiddhi śāstra*) on Buddhist doctrine.

the lender of the goods is like a lord. The borrower is like a pheasant; the lender is like a falcon. But although one may borrow goods, if the lender is excessive in the return he demands, it is he rather than the debtor who will become a horse or an ox and end up serving the borrower. So one should never demand excessive returns.

TALES OF TIMES NOW PAST

KONJAKU MONOGATARI SHŪ

Tales of Times Now Past (*Konjaku monogatari shū*, ca. 1120), a monolithic collection of 1039 *setsuwa*, was compiled in the late Heian period (794–1185). Of the thirty-one books, three (8, 18, and 21) are missing. The collection is divided into three parts: the first five books are on India (*Tenjiku*); the next five books, on China (*Shintan*); and the remaining twenty-one books, on Japan (*Honchō*).

It is not clear whether the compiler was a Buddhist monk or an aristocrat, a single author or a group of writers. Traditionally, the compiler has been thought to be Minamoto no Takakuni (1004–1077), but the inclusion of stories dated after Takakuni's death makes his editorship improbable.

The *Konjaku monogatari shū* is the first world history of Buddhism to have been written in Japanese; two-thirds of the anthology is composed of Buddhist stories and the rest, secular stories. Books 1 through 4 describe the history of Buddhism in India, from the birth of Shakyamuni Buddha to the spread of Buddhism after his death. Books 6 through 9 (8 is missing) cover the transmission of Buddhism from India to China. Books 11 through 20 (18 is missing) outline the history of Buddhism in Japan, beginning with the transmission of Buddhism from China. Finally, books 5, 10, and 21 through 31 (21 is missing) depict secular life in India, China, and Japan. Books 5 and 10—on India and China, respectively—begin with stories about the sovereign and court, followed by stories of ministers and then of warriors. Book 22 provides biographies of powerful Fujiwara ministers, book 23 presents stories of military leaders, and book 24 offers tales of doctors, diviners, and artists. In other words, the secular parts begin with the sovereigns and imperial court as the source of authority and gradually work outward to include such other classes as the samurai, who are featured in book 25. Books 26 through 31 center on the themes of karmic retribution and reward, demons and spirits, humor, and love—depicting a diverse social world that contrasts with the aristocratic world of Heian *monogatari* (court tales).

The *setsuwa* in the *Konjaku monogatari shū* have two large purposes: religious (for leading the audience to a deeper understanding of Buddhism) and secular (for providing entertainment and practical advice). In its religious aims, the *Konjaku monogatari shū* tries to appeal to commoners by presenting Buddhism in a simplified form. The rewards for faith are immediate, and the punishments for sin are direct and immediate. The stories about the Lotus Sutra, for example, make no or little attempt to explain the content of the sutra; instead, they focus on the efficacy and merit acquired by reciting the sutra or having faith in it. Indeed, worldly efficacy—the belief in the power of Buddhism to protect human beings from disasters—is usually stressed. The Buddhist *setsuwa* probably were compiled by Buddhist preachers as a means of instruction for an illiterate audience. They, however, are not sermons but rather stories that could be used in sermons. The moral at the end usually applies to only part of a story, reflecting the multiple functions of these narratives. (Indeed, the same story often appears in another *setsuwa* collection for a completely different purpose.)

The focus of the Buddhist stories generally is on the strange and miraculous rather than on doctrinal matters. The same interest in the strange and mysterious marks the secular books, particularly 27 (demons and spirits), 28 (humor), 29 (evil and criminals), 30 (love stories), and 31 (miscellany of tales). The setting of the *setsuwa* ranges from the ninth to the twelfth century, encompassing the same historical period in which the *monogatari* flourished but with a much broader social and topographical range.

The *Konjaku monogatari shū* was written in *wakan-konkōbun*, a Sino-Japanese style that reflects the Chinese influence of certain sources and a strong movement toward vernacular Japanese. The *setsuwa* are presented not as words directly spoken by the narrator or editor, but as transmissions of stories that have been heard and recorded.

TALES FROM INDIA

Books 1 through 3 begin with the birth of Shakyamuni, the historical Buddha, and end with his death. Book 4 contains stories that take place after Shakyamuni's death, and book 5 focuses on the world before his birth, with stories that overlap with the Jātaka in Pali literature. The stories translated here, from book 5, were chosen because of their impact on Japanese literature.

The story "How the One-Horned Ascetic Carried a Woman on His Back from the Mountains to the Royal City" (5:4), which derives from book 17 of an early-fifth-century Chinese translation from Sanskrit known as *Commentary on the Great Wisdom Sutra* (*Dazhi dulun*, Jp. *Daichidoron*, Skt. *Mahāprajñāpāramitāśāstra*) and is related to a Jātaka story (no. 526). Similar stories appear in book 37 of the *Chronicle of Great Peace* (*Taiheiki*, ca. 1340s–1371) and in numerous *setsuwa* collections, including the early-fifteenth-century *Transmissions from Three Countries* (*Sangoku denki*, 2:28). The "One-Horned Ascetic," which pits ascetic life against erotic lure, became a *nō* play under the same name and, in the mid-eighteenth century, was the basis for the famous kabuki play *Narukami*.

The self-sacrifice of the rabbit in "How Three Beasts Practiced the Bodhisattva Way and How the Rabbit Roasted Himself" (5:13), with the moon to remind us of this great act, reveals the bodhisattva ideal of sacrifice and became famous in Japan. This story is directly linked to the following tale, "How a Lion Showed Pity for a Monkey's Children and Tore Out His Own Flesh for an Eagle" (5:14), which is a parable about the sacrifice of Shakyamuni Buddha.

The story "How a Nine-Colored Deer Came Out of a Mountain and Saved a Man from Drowning" (5:18), which is associated with a Jātaka tale (no. 482), is a noted example of an *ongaeshi* (repaying-gratitude tale), which was to become a major narrative pattern in Japanese *setsuwa* and folklore. Typically, an animal (such as a snake, fox, turtle, frog, or crab) saves a human being, who does not forget the gratitude or obligation. In this story, the *ongaeshi* is combined with the concept of *hōjō* (liberation of sentient beings).

✳

How the One-Horned Ascetic Carried a Woman on His Back from the Mountains to the Royal City (5:4)

Long ago in India, there was a *sennin*, or mountain ascetic.[1] He was called the One-Horned Ascetic because he had a single horn growing out of his forehead. He had lived for many years deep in the mountains, devoting himself to religious practices. He could ride on the clouds and soar through the sky, move lofty mountains and make birds and beasts obey his commands.

It so happened that torrential rains suddenly began to fall, and all the trails were reduced to a wretched condition. The ascetic was for some reason powerless to deal with such circumstances. For lack of any better alternative, he tried making his way on foot, but the mountains were so steep that he kept slipping and falling down. He was well along in years, and when he fell down in this way, it made him extremely angry. "It's because it keeps on raining here in the world that the trails are in such wretched shape and I fall down like this!" he said. "My robes of moss are sopping and have a nasty feel to them. It's the dragon kings who are causing all this rain!" He then pounced on the dragon kings and stuffed them into the water bottle he was carrying. The dragon kings were extremely grieved and unhappy about this.

Big as they were, the dragon kings had been stuffed into a very narrow space and were unable to move, which distressed them greatly. But because the ascetic was a holy man and wielded highly esteemed powers, there was nothing they could do about this. Thus time went by, until for twenty years no rain whatsoever had fallen. As a result, the whole world was afflicted with drought, and all the five lands of India were plunged into endless grief.

1. The *sennin* were ascetics who lived in the mountains, practicing religious austerities and hoping to attain immortal life. According to the Indian legend from which this story is taken, a certain mountain ascetic, observing two deer copulating, became sexually excited and spilled his semen. The doe then lapped up the semen, became pregnant, and in time gave birth to the One-Horned Ascetic. He had the feet of a deer and a horn on his forehead.

The kings of the sixteen great states of India carried out various prayers and petitions, begging the rain to fall, but even these had no effect. The kings were at their wit's end and had no idea what to do.

At that point, a certain soothsayer said to the kings, "To the northeast of here is a tall mountain, and in the mountain lives an ascetic. He has seized all the dragon kings who cause the rain to fall and placed them in confinement—that's why no rain falls in the world. Your holy men may offer all the prayers they like, but they can never compete with the power of that holy man in the mountain!"

When the people of the various lands heard this, they tried to come up with some plan of action, but could think of nothing. Then one of the high officials said, "He may be a holy man, and that's our hard luck. But there's never been anyone who was blind to physical beauty or uncharmed by sweet voices. Long ago there was an ascetic named Udraka Ramaputra who was much more advanced in powers than this mountain man. But he suddenly fell under the spell of feminine allure and lost all his mystical powers. So we should try that approach. Let a call be sent out to recruit all the women in the sixteen great states who are outstanding in beauty and have charming voices. We'll send them into the mountain, to the lofty peaks and deep valleys, wherever this ascetic dwells, where this holy man makes his quarters. And then, when they sing their plaintive and seductive songs, then, holy man though he may be, he cannot fail to succumb to them!"

"That's what we'll do, starting at once!" his listeners exclaimed, and they set out to round up women of superb beauty and alluring voices from the population. When they had selected five hundred such women, they decked them in attractive garments, scented them with sandalwood perfume, bathed them in aloe-scented water, placed them in five hundred elegantly adorned carriages, and sent them off.

The women entered the mountain, stepped down from their carriages, and all five hundred of them, flocking together, walked this way and that. What a splendid sight they were! Then they separated, walking in groups of ten or twenty individuals. They made their way among the various caves, through the trees, and between the mountain peaks, singing their songs in a plaintive manner. The mountains echoed with them, the valleys resounded, and the heavenly beings, the dragons and gods, gathered around to listen.

Presently, standing beside a deep cavern, wearing robes made of moss, the holy man himself appeared. Lean, emaciated, there was scarcely any flesh on his body. Nothing but skin and bones, one might wonder where his spirit had any room to hide. From his forehead grew his single horn. He was an unspeakably weird and frightening sight. A mere shadow of a being, he leaned on his staff, clasping his water bottle, and with a wry smile on his face came hobbling forward.

"What sort of beings are you, that you appear here and favor me with the singing of these splendid songs? I have lived in this mountain now for a thousand years, but I have never heard their like before. Are you beings come down from heaven, or minions of the devil pressing in on me?" asked the holy man.

Then one of the women replied, "We are not heavenly beings, nor minions of the devil. We are five hundred Kekara[2] women who, banding together as a group, have come here from India. We heard that this was a mountain of unparalleled appeal, where ten thousand flowers bloom, where streams flow most bountifully, and that herein dwells a saint matchless in holiness. We will sing songs for him, we thought, for if he resides in the mountains, he has doubtless never heard songs such as ours. And in that way, we can form a religious bond with him. For these reasons, therefore, we have made a point of coming here!"

When the holy man listened to their songs, beholding a sight such as he had never seen in past or present, singing that was plaintive and seductive, his eyes were dazed, his emotions stirred, his heart was deeply moved, and his spirit led quite astray.

"Would you be kind enough to heed my request?" asked the holy man.

The woman assumed an inviting air, thinking that in that way she could entrap him. "What would you like me to do? What request could I fail to comply with?" she said.

"I thought if I could touch you—perhaps just a little—," said the holy man, speaking in a gruff and awkward manner.

2. Kekara is probably a corruption of the word Gandhara, a region in modern Pakistan.

The woman was terrified, but at the same time did not wish to offend him. There he was, that ugly horn growing out of his head, yet she had been sent by the kings with specific instructions to treat him kindly. In the end, therefore, frightening as it was, she let the holy man do as he had requested.

At that moment, the dragon kings, filled with joy, came bursting out of the water bottle and rose up into the air.[3] No sooner had they done so than the whole sky darkened and clouded over, thunder rumbled, lightning flashed, and heavy rain began to fall.

The woman had no place to hide, but neither could she make her way out of the mountain. Therefore, terrified though she was, she remained where she was during the days that followed.

The holy man meanwhile had fallen deeply in love with her. When five days had passed, he said, "The rain has let up and the sky is clearing."

"I can't stay here any longer," the woman said to the holy man. "I must be starting back."

Reluctant to part with her, the holy man said, "Well, I suppose you must," but he spoke in a distressed and doleful manner.

"I'm not used to a place like this," said the woman. "Walking over these rocky cliffs, my feet are all bruised and swollen. And on top of that, I don't know which is the way home!"

"In that case," said the holy man, "I will act as your guide on the road out of the mountains."

He started out ahead of her. And as she looked at him—head as though mantled in snow, face all in wrinkles, his one horn growing out of his forehead, bent over at the waist, dressed in robes of moss, leaning on his pewter-ringed staff,[4] and tottering along—she thought she had never seen anyone so ridiculous, and at the same time so frightening.

After a while, they came to a place where the trail was no more than a thin ledge running along the side of the mountain. Sheer cliffs rose on

---

3. The holy man has revealed himself as subject to sensual desires, and hence his magical powers have deserted him.

4. Walking sticks topped with pewter rings were standard accoutrements of Buddhist monks who traveled in the mountains. The clatter of the rings was intended to scare away noxious creatures in the path of the walker.

either side, like a pair of folding screens, with huge waterfalls tumbling down them. Below was a deep pool from which white waves leaped up as though about to climb back into the air. Everywhere one looked were dense banks of cloud and mist. In fact, unless one sprouted wings or climbed on a dragon's back, it was hard to imagine how one could possibly get past such a place.

When the woman reached the spot, she said to the holy man, "I don't see how I can go on. Just looking at it, my eyes grow dim and I don't even know what I'm doing. How could I possibly make my way ahead? But you are accustomed to walking such trails. Perhaps you could carry me on your back."

The holy man was so deeply infatuated with her that he felt he could not refuse. "All right," he said. "Here—climb on my back." His legs were so spindly they looked as though they were about to snap, and he was terrified that he might drop her, but he carried her on his back nevertheless. When they got past the difficult place, the woman said, "Just a little farther!" and in this way she got him to carry her all the way to the royal city.

When the pair were spotted on the road and word got around that the holy man One-Horned Ascetic who lived in the mountains was entering the capital carrying a Kekara woman on his back, people from all over the broad land of India, those high and low in station, men and women alike, gathered around to have a look. There he was, his one horn growing out of his forehead, his head as though mantled in snow. His legs were thin as needles, and he used his pewter-ringed staff to hold up the woman's rear end, jacking her up when she threatened to slip down his back. No one could keep from laughing and jeering at them.

When they entered the royal palace, the king too was moved to laughter. But he had heard that the holy man was highly venerated and so he treated him with respect and awe. "Hurry now, return to where you came from!" he said. And the holy man, who up to now had felt as though he were flying through the air, staggering, stumbling, made his way back home. Accounts tell us there really was a holy man as ridiculous as this!

How Three Beasts Practiced the Bodhisattva Way and How the Rabbit Roasted Himself (5:13)

Once long ago in India there were three beasts—a rabbit, a fox, and a monkey—who together determined to seek enlightenment and devote themselves to the bodhisattva way. Each thought to himself, "Because in our previous existences we incurred a heavy burden of guilt, we have been reborn in this lowly form as beasts. In our former lives, we showed no pity for living beings, were stingy with our goods and wealth, and gave nothing to others. Because of these grave offenses, we fell into hell and suffered there a long time, and since a residue of guilt still remained, we were condemned to be born in our present form. But now we must rid ourselves of these animal bodies!"

To those older in years, they showed the respect due to parents; those only a little older they treated as older brothers; and with those younger, they displayed the affection one would for a younger brother. They set aside their own concerns and thought first of the concerns of others.

The god Indra[5] took note of this. "Although beasts in body," he said, "they have set their minds on a noble goal. Yet even among those born in human form are some who kill living creatures, seize the goods belonging to others, murder their own father or mother, or treat their elder or younger brothers with enmity. Some hide evil designs behind a smiling face; some feign affection while nursing deep anger in their hearts. It seems hardly likely, then, that these beasts should in truth entertain such exalted aims. I must put them to a test!"

So saying, he abruptly transformed himself into an old man, feeble, helpless, with no visible means of support. Then he went to the three beasts and said, "I'm an old man, feeble, helpless. You three beasts, please

---

5. A major figure in the ancient Indian pantheon, Indra is the god of thunder and rain. He was later incorporated into Buddhism as a guardian deity.

help me! I have no children, my house is poor, and I've nothing to eat! I have heard that you three show deep pity in your hearts."

When the three beasts heard this, they said, "This is exactly what we had hoped for. We will look to your needs at once!"

Then the monkey, climbing trees, picked chestnuts, persimmons, pears, jujubes, tangerines, oranges, monkey pears, hazelnuts, and two kinds of *akebi* fruit and brought them around. Going out to the village fields, he gathered melons, eggplants, beans, adzuki beans, black-eyed peas, foxtail millet, panic grass, and Chinese millet and brought these, too, preparing them to the old man's taste.

The fox went off to the graveyard where people had put out offerings of food; gathered up the rice cakes and other rice dishes and the abalone, bonito, and similar kinds of seafood; and brought them, fixing them in a suitable manner. By this time, the old man had eaten all he could eat.

After a few days had passed in this way, the old man said, "You two beasts have hearts that are truly fine! Already you've shown yourselves to be bodhisattvas!"

The rabbit, inspired by these words, seized a torch and some oil, pricked up his ears, arched his back, opened his eyes, pulled in his paws, and with the hole in his rear end wide open, rushed off east and west, north and south, hunting for something to eat. But no matter where he looked, he could find nothing. Meanwhile, the monkey, the fox, and the old man cried "Shame!" berating him, or tried to encourage him with smiles, but all in vain.

The rabbit thought to himself, "To find food for this old man I could go off to the fields and mountains, but the fields and mountains are a fearful place, there's nothing to be found there! I'd only be killed by human beings or by other beasts. I'd never accomplish my aim but would lose my life for nothing. If I am to cast off my present form, better that I do so once and for all by being eaten by this old man!"

Then he went to where the old man was and said, "I've looked around and found something delicious for you to eat! Gather some wood and prepare a fire to cook it with!"

The monkey then gathered some firewood, and the fox got a fire going, waiting and wondering what the rabbit would bring. But the rabbit came with nothing at all.

When the monkey and the fox saw this, they said, "What have you brought? Just as we suspected—it was all a lying scheme! You wanted us to gather wood and make a fire simply so you could warm yourself by the flames! How hateful!"

The rabbit said, "I looked for something to eat but couldn't find anything. So I'll just provide food by roasting my own body!" And with these words, he leaped into the fire and burned to death.

Then the god Indra, changing back into his original form, took the body of the rabbit out of the flames and placed it in the moon. He did this so that all living beings everywhere could look at it and remember. Thus it is that when something like clouds veil the face of the moon, this is smoke from the fire in which the rabbit burned himself. And when people talk about a rabbit in the moon, it is the body of this rabbit they mean. Whenever people anywhere look at the moon, let them remember the rabbit's story.

How a Lion Showed Pity for a Monkey's Children and Tore Out His Own Flesh for an Eagle (5:14)

Long ago in India, there was a lion who lived in a cave deep in the mountains. This lion thought to himself, "I am the king of the beasts. Therefore, I must guard and look out for the other beasts."

There were some monkeys living in this mountain, a husband and a wife, and they became parents to two little monkeys who in time grew to be big monkeys. While the baby monkeys were still little, one of the parents would clasp a baby to its stomach and the other would carry a baby on its back, and in this way they would range over the mountain fields, gathering fruits and berries to feed the babies. But when the babies got bigger, it was no longer possible to clasp them to their stomachs or carry them on their backs. Hence the parents could no longer range over the mountain fields, gathering fruits and berries, and no longer had any way to feed their offspring. And, in fact, they found it hard even to prolong their own lives. Because if they left their offspring at home and went off in search of food, they feared that birds might swoop down from the sky and eat their little ones, or other beasts might rush in and make off with them. Beset by worries of this kind, they remained where they were until they were exhausted and on the verge of starvation.

Trying to come up with some solution to this problem, they thought to themselves, "In a cave in this mountain lives a lion. If we get the lion to look after these children of ours, we can go out to the mountain fields, gather fruits and berries to feed the children, and at the same time prolong our own lives."

With this thought in mind, they went to the cave and said to the lion, "The lion is the king of the beasts. Therefore, it is up to him first of all to pity and take care of the other beasts. We too are beasts, lowly though we are, and so deserve your pity. We have given birth to two children. While they were still little, we would carry one on our back and have the other cling to our stomach, and in that way go out to the mountain fields to gather fruits and berries to feed the children and sustain our own lives.

"But since the children have bit by bit grown bigger, it's no longer possible to carry them on our backs or clinging to our stomachs, and we can't go out into the fields as we used to. So both our children and we ourselves are about to die of starvation. If we left the children alone and went off to look for food, we are fearful of what the other beasts might do. Hence we don't dare do that, though we are on the verge of starvation. But perhaps, while we go off to the mountain fields to gather fruits and berries, we could leave the children with you, and you would be kind enough to look after them. Then, knowing they were in your care, we would feel completely at ease."

"What you say is quite reasonable," the lion replied. "Bring the children at once and leave them here. I will look out for them until you come back."

The monkeys were delighted with the lion's answer, brought their children, and left them with him while they went off to the mountain fields to gather fruits and berries, no longer a worry in mind.

The lion placed the two little monkeys in front of him and, never once looking aside, proceeded to guard them. But then he fell into a doze, and at that moment an eagle came and hid in a tree at the mouth of the cave. "If he lets down his guard for a moment, I can grab those monkeys and make off with them," he thought to himself. And when he saw that the lion had dozed off, he flew down, seized one monkey in each of his claws, and returned with them to the tree so he could devour them.

The lion, startled, looked around in alarm but could see no sign of the monkeys. In alarm, he rushed out of the cave, and there he saw the eagle in the nearby tree, pinning the monkeys down with both of his claws and preparing to eat them.

Panicked at the sight of this, he advanced to the tree and addressed the eagle: "You are the king of the birds; I, the king of the beasts. We ought to have a little consideration for one another. Some monkeys who live in the vicinity of this cave came to me and said that they have to go out to gather fruits and berries to feed their offspring and to keep themselves alive. But they were worried what might become of their two offspring when they went out to the mountain fields, and so they asked me to look out for them and left them in my cave. But now you wait until I doze off a little and come and snatch them away. Please be good enough to give them back! I promised I would guard them, and if I were to fail to keep my promise, it would be as though my very liver and heart were cut out! So I'm sure you will not refuse my request. If I get really angry and begin to roar, things will not be so pleasant for you and the others around here!"

"What you say is quite right," the eagle replied. "But I intend to make these two monkeys my meal for today. If I returned them to you, I would be in danger of starving this very day. I have the greatest respect for your concerns as a lion, but I must think of my own welfare. Therefore, I cannot obey your wishes, for that would jeopardize my own survival."

"The explanation you give is entirely reasonable," said the lion.

"That being the case, let me offer you a portion of my own flesh to use in place of the two monkeys. Let that serve as your meal for today." Then, with his claws sharp as swords, he tore a piece of flesh from his thigh, equal in size to the two monkeys put together, and presented it to the eagle. Then he asked the eagle to return the monkeys. "In view of the circumstances," said the eagle, "what reason would I have to refuse?" and he handed them over.

Having regained possession of the two monkeys, the lion, his body covered in blood, returned to his cave. When the mother monkey came back from gathering fruits and berries and heard from the lion what had happened, her tears fell like rain. "I was not so much concerned about you in particular," the lion said to her. "But I had given my promise, and I would have been profoundly disturbed to think that I had not been true to it. And then, too, it is my duty to show deep pity for all beasts!"

The lion was the one we now know as Shakyamuni. The father monkey was the Venerable Kashyapa and the mother monkey was the nun Zengo. The two little monkeys were Ānanda and Rāhula. The eagle was ——. This is the tale that has been told.[6]

How a Nine-Colored Deer Came Out of a Mountain and Saved a Man from Drowning (5:18)

Long ago in India there was a mountain, and in this mountain lived a deer who had nine colors adorning his body and white horns. The people of the country did not know that he lived in the mountains. In front of the mountain was a great river. In this mountain there also lived a crow, and it and the deer had passed many years together, one in mind.

Now there was a man who set out to cross the river, but he was swept off his feet, bobbing and sinking. He thought that he would surely die, when he managed to grab onto a floating log. As he drifted along, he called out, "You mountain gods, you forest gods, heavenly beings, dragon gods, why don't you save me?" But no matter how he cried, no one came to help him.

As it happened, however, the deer who lived in the mountain had just then come down to the river. Hearing his cries, he said to the man, "Don't be afraid—I'll carry you on my back. Take hold of my two horns, and I'll put you on my back and take you to the shore!" And he swam across the river and helped the man to reach the embankment.

---

6. Kashyapa, Ānanda, and Rāhula were among the ten major disciples of Shakyamuni Buddha. Ānanda was a cousin of the Buddha, and Rāhula was the Buddha's son. The identity of the nun Zengo is unknown. There is a blank in the text where one would expect to learn the identity of the eagle, presumably because the writer intended at some point to gather further information or deliberately left a blank.

The nine-colored deer kneels in front of the king's carriage. (From an Edo-period wood-block edition of *Uji shūi monogatari*, with the permission of Komine Kazuaki)

The man, overjoyed at having his life saved, faced the deer, bowed to him, and, weeping, said, "That I am alive today is due solely to your help. How can I repay the debt I owe you?"

The deer said, "What is this talk of repaying a debt? I only ask that you never, never tell anyone that I live in this mountain. My body is adorned with nine colors—like no other in this world—and my horns are white as snow. If people learn of this, they will want to get hold of my hide and horns and will surely kill me. That is what I fear, and so I hide deep in this mountain and let no one know I am here. I beg you, dim your voice, summon up a heart of deep pity, and help me!"

The man, moved by the deer's pleas, weeping copiously, again and again replied that he would tell no one what had happened, and so they parted.

The man returned to his native village, and though the days and months passed by, he never spoke a word of what had happened to anyone. At that time, however, the consort of the ruler of the kingdom told of what she had seen in a dream: a huge deer, his body adorned with nine colors and with white horns. After the dream had ended, she fell ill, driven by a desire to gain possession of the colorful deer.

When the ruler of the kingdom asked her why she did not get up, she explained, "I have seen that colorful deer in a dream, just as it is, and so I know it must exist in this world. I must get it, strip it of its hide, and get its horns!" The king accordingly issued a proclamation, saying, "If there is anyone who has knowledge of such-and-such a deer, let him come forward—he shall be given gold, silver, and other treasures. Whatever he asks for, he shall receive!" Such was the proclamation.

At that time, when the man who had been helped by the deer heard the proclamation, he was seized with desires in his heart that he could not repress, and he forgot what he had promised the deer. He said to the king, "In such-and-such a country, in such-and-such a mountain, you will find him—that deer of nine colors! I know where he is. Quickly prepare your forces, and I will take you there!"

The king was delighted when he heard this. "I will lead out my forces, and we will set off for that mountain!" he said, and at once gave orders for a large force to be called out, and they headed for the mountain. He appointed the man to act as guide to show them the way. They had already entered the mountain, but the nine-colored deer, having no word whatsoever of their coming, slept soundly in the fastness of his lair.

At that moment the crow, his bosom friend, seeing the troops advancing, flew to the deer's lair in alarm and confusion, screeching loudly to warn him. Addressing the deer, he said, "Because the great king of this land wants to use your colored hide, he has led out many troops and surrounded this valley. Even now, though you flee, it is too late to save your life!" Having delivered his message, he flew away lamenting.

The deer, startled, looked about and saw that the great king had led many of his forces and surrounded him. Realizing that there was no chance of fleeing, he decided to walk right up to the king's carriage. The armed men all cocked their bows in preparation to shoot.

At that time, the king gave an order: "You men, for the present do nothing to harm this deer. Looking at it, I can see that his hide is not like that of an ordinary deer. He has shown no fear of my forces, but has approached my carriage. Let us wait and see what he will do." With this, the troops put down their weapons and waited.

The deer knelt in front of the royal carriage and spoke: "I, because of fear for my colored hide, have for many years now lived in hiding in the deep valleys, never daring to let anyone know where I was. Great king, how have you learned of my whereabouts?"

The king replied, "I knew nothing of your whereabouts. It was this man by my carriage, the one with a birthmark on his face, who told me of it."

The deer, hearing the king's explanation, turned to look at the man by the carriage side. He had a birthmark on his face, and was the man whom he had helped.

Facing the man when he spoke, he said, "When I saved your life, I was happy to do you that favor, and you promised over and over again never to tell anyone about my whereabouts. Why have you forgotten your mercy and now tell the king to put me to death? When you were on the point of drowning, I forgot about the dangers to my life and swam out to help you, steering you into the shore. Now to forget that kindness—this is a deed of unmitigated evil!" The tears flowed down as he wept uncontrollably. Faced with the deer's accusation, the man had nothing to say.

Then the king spoke up. "From this day forward, let no man within this realm venture to kill a deer! If anyone violates this commandment and ventures to kill even one deer, he shall be put to death and his house destroyed!" said the king. Then he led his forces back to the capital. The deer, too, went home happy.

From that time on, the rains in the state fell in season and no intemperate winds blew. The realm was without pestilence, the five grains grew in abundance, and there were no poor people.

Hence we know that among humans there are those who forget about a deed of kindness, while among the beasts there are those who save human beings. Present and past, it has been ever so. According to tradition, that deer with the nine-colored hide was the one we know as Shakyamuni Buddha. The crow who understood his heart was Ānanda. The king's consort was the one known as Sundarī. The man who came near to drowning was the present-day Devadatta.[7]

TALES FROM CHINA

Books 6 through 9, which cover the transmission of Buddhism from India to China, include various stories of miracles and karmic causality. Book 6 begins with the suppression of Buddhism under the First Emperor (r. 246–221 B.C.E.) of China, while book 7 depicts the world after death and hell, which are rarely revealed in the Indian tales. Book 9, which includes the story "How Moye of China Made a Sword and Presented It to the King and How His Son, Broad-of-Brow, Was Killed" (9:44),[8] focuses on stories of filial piety, which were important not only for Confucianism but also for Buddhism. Book 10 is a secular history (*kokushi*) of China that begins

---

7. Ānanda was a cousin of Shakyamuni Buddha and an important disciple. Sundarī was the woman who slandered Shakyamuni and caused the followers to doubt his word. Devadatta was a close disciple of Shakyamuni who later turned against him.

8. For an analysis of the tale, see Michelle Osterfeld Li, *Ambiguous Bodies: Reading the Grotesque in Japanese Setsuwa Tales* (Stanford, Calif.: Stanford University Press, 2009), 57–65.

with a mini-history of the First Emperor and includes the tale "How Wang Zhaojun, Consort of Emperor Yuan of the Han, Went to the Land of the Hu" (10:5). The story of Wang Zhaojun, a woman whose legend became famous in China, appears repeatedly in Japanese literature.

How Moye of China Made a Sword and Presented It to the King and How His Son, Broad-of-Brow, Was Killed (9:44)

Long ago in China in the reign of King ——,[9] there lived a man named Moye who was an ironworker by trade.

At that time, the king's consort, unable to bear the summer heat, was constantly to be found clinging to the iron stanchions of the palace. Later she gave birth to a child. (She clung to them because they were cool.)

The king, wondering at her behavior, asked her, "Why do you do that?" The queen replied, "I'm doing nothing wrong. It's just that the summer heat is intolerable, so I cling to the iron stanchions. Is there something odd in that?"

"So that's the reason," thought the king. He summoned Moye, who had made the iron stanchions, and ordered him to fashion a precious sword.

When Moye came to make the sword, he decided to fashion two of them, one to present to the king and one to put aside and keep secret. When the king had duly received the sword that Moye had made for him, he discovered that the sword was constantly lamenting. The king, wondering at this, questioned his high ministers. "Why is the sword crying?" he asked them.

The high ministers replied, "There's bound to be some reason why the sword cries. Perhaps it's because this is one of two swords, a husband and a wife. If so, then it cries out its love for the other."

The king, hearing this, was extremely angry. Summoning Moye at once, he berated him for his fault in the matter.

9. Although there is a blank in the text rather than a name, the story of Moye and his sword or swords in Chinese sources traditionally has been associated with King Helu (r. 514–496 B.C.E.) of the state of Wu.

But even before the messenger arrived from the king summoning him, Moye had been talking with his wife: "Tonight I have a very inauspicious feeling. A messenger from the king is certain to come. I know I cannot escape the death penalty! If the child in your womb is a boy, then, when he grows up, tell him, 'Look among the pines of the southern mountain!'"

That night he left by the northern door, hid himself among the great trees of the southern mountain, and in time died there.

After that, his wife bore a son. When he was fifteen years of age, the space between his eyes measured one foot—hence he was called Broad-of-Brow. His mother repeated to him all the sayings that the father had left behind, and the son followed the instructions of the mother. She gave him the sword, for she had come to believe that he was destined to carry out vengeance for his father's death.

At the time, the king had a dream in which someone who measured a foot between his eyes was plotting to revolt and kill him. When the king awoke, he was full of fear and alarm and immediately dispatched an order to all four quarters, saying, "There is in the world someone who measures a foot from eye to eye. Seize him and bring him to me! To anyone who brings me his head, I will give a thousand gold pieces as a reward!"

At that time, when Broad-of-Brow came to hear of this, he fled into hiding deep in the mountains. The messengers bearing the king's proclamation searched everywhere in the four directions, and one of them happened to come upon Broad-of-Brow in the mountains. When he looked, he could see that he measured a foot from eye to eye. Filled with delight, he said, "Are you the man called Broad-of-Brow?" "I am," replied Broad-of-Brow. "I and the others bear a royal proclamation," he said. "We are searching for your head and for the sword that you bear."

Hearing this, Broad-of-Brow took the sword and, cutting off his own head, presented it to the envoy. The envoy took the head and, returning, handed it to the king. The king was delighted and rewarded the envoy.

After this, Broad-of-Brow's head having been delivered by the envoy, the king declared, "We must quickly demolish it by boiling it!" But when the envoy, following the king's instructions, put the head in a cauldron of boiling water, it sat there for seven days without showing any signs of disintegrating.

The king, thinking this very strange and attempting to discover the reason, went and peered into the cauldron, whereupon the king's head fell off of its own volition and dropped into the water. The two heads seemed to be fighting with each other, with no end to the struggle. The envoy, thinking this highly peculiar, in an attempt to weaken the struggles of Broad-of Brow's head, tried sticking the sword into the cauldron. When he did this, both the heads began to fester. But while the envoy was peering into the cauldron, his own head fell off and dropped into the water. Thus there were three heads in the water, all run together so that it was impossible to distinguish them. As a result, all three heads were buried in a single grave.

That grave is said to be still in existence, located, I am told, in the district of Yishun.

How Wang Zhaojun, Consort of Emperor Yuan of the Han, Went to the Land of the Hu (10:5)

Long ago, in the reign of Emperor Yuan [r. 48–33 B.C.E.] of the Han dynasty in China, the emperor commanded that, from among the daughters of the high ministers and nobles, those of outstanding beauty of face and form be selected, and that all of them be brought to the imperial palace. The women numbered some four or five hundred, so many that, as it turned out later, the emperor could not necessarily get to know each one individually.

At that time, some men from the land of the Hu had appeared in the capital, persons of a barbarian nature.[10] The emperor himself, along with the high ministers and the various other government officials, pondered what to do about this troubling situation but could come up with no good plan.

---

10. The land of the Hu refers to the area north of China occupied by the Xiongnu, a non-Chinese nomadic people who at times posed a severe military threat to China. The story refers to events in 33 B.C.E., when the leader of the Xiongnu and his entourage paid a visit to the Han court at Chang'an.

Then one wise man among the high ministers came forward with this suggestion. "The fact that these men of Hu have come here is highly injurious to the interests of our country," he said. "To ensure that they return to their own country, I would suggest that, since there are so many more women in the palace than are needed, one woman of inferior looks be selected from among these and handed over to the Hu country people. If so, they will surely be pleased and will go back home. I believe there can be no better plan than this."

When the emperor heard this suggestion, he said, "Very well!" But when it came to inspecting the women in person and selecting one, he realized that, there being so many of them, it would be quite troublesome. Instead, he decided to summon a number of painters and have them examine the women and paint portraits of them. Then he could look over the portraits and pick one woman of inferior features to give to the Hu people.

And so the painters began their portraits. The women, filled with alarm and sorrow at the thought that one of them was to become the plaything of a barbarian and journey to a distant and unknown land, vied with one another to offer the painters gifts of gold and silver or other goods of value. The painters, beguiled by such gifts, accordingly painted even the ungainly ones in an attractive manner, and the portraits were then presented to the emperor.

There was one among the women named Wang Zhaojun, who as a matter of fact outshone all the others in beauty of form. But she relied on her beauty and did not offer the painter anything in the way of a bribe. As a result, he did not paint her features as they actually were, but portrayed her as extremely unattractive. And when her portrait was presented, the decision was made: "We'll send this one!"

The emperor, wondering about this decision, summoned Wang Zhaojun to appear before him. Her beauty shone like a beam of light; she was a veritable jewel beside the other women, who were so much mud. The emperor, astounded, grieved to think of handing her over to the barbarians. But as the days went by, the barbarians heard reports that Wang Zhaojun was to be given to them, and they appeared at the palace to make inquiries. It was impossible to reverse the decision, and so in the end Wang

Zhaojun was handed over to the Hu people. Mounting a horse, she set off on her journey to the land of the Hu.

Wang Zhaojun wept in sorrow, but she knew there was nothing that could be done. The emperor too, deeply saddened, thought of her with longing. So deep were his thoughts that he visited the places where she had once been. In spring, the branches of the willows swayed in the breeze, the warblers singing in vain in them. With autumn, the fallen leaves of the trees piled up in the courtyard, where the ferns that cling to the eaves wakened endless sad memories. No words could describe the scene, and it only deepened his grief and longing.

The men of Hu, having acquired Wang Zhaojun, were delighted and, playing various tunes on their lutes, set off on the journey. As she listened to them, Wang Zhaojun, amid her tears and lamentations, felt a little bit comforted. Once they arrived in Hu, she became the consort of the ruler and was treated with the highest honor. But in her heart, this could hardly make up for what had happened. All this came about because she relied on her good looks and failed to bribe the painter. And the people of the time, we are told, blamed her for that.

✸

BUDDHIST TALES OF JAPAN

Books 11 through 21, which outline the history of Buddhism in Japan, beginning with the transmission of Buddhism from China, include stories about Prince Shōtoku (574–622). Books 13 and 14 describe miracles associated with the Lotus Sutra or the reading of the Lotus Sutra. For example, "How a Monk of Dōjō-ji in Kii Province Copied the Lotus Sutra and Brought Salvation to the Snakes" (14:3)[11] claims to prove the efficacy and power of the Lotus Sutra. In typical Mahayana fashion, the story stresses the need for such intermediaries and the fact that even the most evil can

---

11. Dōjō-ji is an ancient Buddhist temple on the seacoast in Kii Province, present-day Wakayama Prefecture. The story relates the legend for which the temple has long been famous.

be saved by Buddhism. But the actual interest of the story, which had a profound influence on Japanese literature and drama and appears in many variants, extends far beyond this didactic ending to explore the large issues of gender and amorous attachment.

The stories of miracles related to Kannon (Avalokiteśvara), the bodhisattva of mercy, described in book 16 are followed, in book 17, by stories of miracles associated with various deities and bodhisattvas, particularly Jizō. A compelling example is "How Kaya no Yoshifuji of Bitchū Province Became the Husband of a Fox and Was Saved by Kannon" (16:17), a *setsuwa* that reveals the power of Kannon and takes up the theme of attachment, which is blinding and deceiving. In this tale, as elsewhere, the Buddhist message evinces profound skepticism about external appearances and warns us not to be deluded.

Book 19 includes tales of spiritual awakenings and other Buddhist-related stories. A noted example is "How Ōe no Sadamoto, Governor of Mikawa, Became a Buddhist Monk" (19:2). This tale, which also appears in *A Collection of Tales from Uji* (*Uji shūi monogatari*, 52 and 172), actually consists of two conversion stories. In the first, the attachment to his beloved causes a man to sleep with her dead body until the putrefaction awakens him. In the second, the pheasants that are butchered while alive awaken the protagonist. The *setsuwa* ends with a tale of good works, in which a dirty beggar turns out to be the bodhisattva Monju (Mañjuśri), whose identity is revealed by the purple cloud. The last part describes the virtuous acts of Jakushō, who created a bath for commoners.

Book 20 contains tales about *tengu* (literally, "heavenly dog"), the long-nosed, red-faced goblins with mysterious powers; stories about the revival of the dead; and *setsuwa* about karmic rebirth and retribution in this world. The *tengu* and other demonic figures prevent devotion to and understanding of the Buddhist ideals, such as the Three Treasures.[12] A good example is "How a Palace Guard of the Takiguchi Unit Went to Collect Gold During the Reign of Emperor Yōzei" (20:10). In this story, which also appears in the *Uji shūi monogatari* (106), the protagonist is lured and victimized by

---

12. The Three Treasures of Buddhism are the Buddha, the doctrine, and the monastic order or, in more general terms, the community of believers.

heretical, magical cults and by deceptive, magical creatures such as a huge serpent and a gigantic wild boar.

How a Monk of Dōjō-ji in Kii Province Copied the Lotus Sutra and Brought Salvation to the Snakes (14:3)

Long ago, there were two monks who went on a pilgrimage to the Kumano shrines.[13] One was an old man; the other was young, a strikingly handsome figure. When they reached the district of Muro, they asked at a private house for lodging for the two of them for the night. The owner of the house was a young single woman, with two or three women servants.

When the woman of the house saw how handsome the young monk lodger was, her heart was stirred by deep feelings of love and desire, and she treated him with special care.

When night came and the two monks had gone to bed, the woman of the house around midnight made her way to where the young monk was sleeping, removed her clothes, and, placing them over the two of them, lay down beside him. Then she woke him up.

The monk, waking and realizing the situation, was troubled and alarmed. "I ordinarily never give lodging to others," the woman said. "I agreed to put you up tonight because, from the time I first caught sight of you today, I determined deep in my heart that I'd make you my husband. I gave you lodging so I could achieve that aim. That's why I've come here. I have no husband; I'm single. Have pity on me!"

When the monk heard this, he was deeply disturbed and, sitting up in bed, said to her, "Because of a vow taken in the past, I have for some time kept myself pure in body and mind and have set out on this journey to pay my respects at the sacred shrines of the deities present here.[14] If I were

---

13. The Kumano shrines are three old and important Shinto shrines in the mountains of Kii Province. They were also a center of Buddhist devotion.

14. The monk is referring to the Shinto and Buddhist deities of the Kumano shrines.

suddenly to violate my vow, it would have fearful consequences for us both! You must give up this idea at once!" He was adamant in his refusals.

The woman, deeply angered, continued all night to cling to the monk, attempting to force or entice him to her will. The monk tried various ways to calm and appease her. "It is not that I refuse your offer," he said. "But I'm on my way now to Kumano. In two or three days, after I have made my offerings of lamps and paper strips,[15] I will return this way again and comply with your proposal." Such was the promise he made, and she, relying on this promise, returned to her own room. When dawn came, the two monks left the house and continued on their way to Kumano.

From then on, the woman, counting on the promised day, put all other concerns out of her mind and, longing only for the monk, busied herself with various preparations, waiting for his return. As for the two monks, when the time came to return, because of their fear of the woman, they did not pass by her house but hurried off in a quite different direction and thus escaped.

The woman, wondering why the monks were so long in coming and weary of waiting, went out into the road and questioned the people passing by. One of them was a monk returning from Kumano. She asked him if two monks, one young and one old, dressed in robes of such and such a color, had started on their way back. "Those two monks started back some time ago—it's been two or three days by now," he replied. When the woman heard this, she clapped her hands in alarm. "He's taken some other road and escaped!" she thought to herself. Deeply incensed, she returned to her house and shut herself up in the bedroom. No sound was heard, but after a while it was found that she had died.

Her women attendants, seeing this, began weeping and lamenting, whereupon a poisonous snake five arm-spans in length suddenly emerged from the bedroom. It went out of the house and headed for the road, as though intending to follow the route taken by those returning from Kumano. When people saw this, they were terrified.

The two monks, meanwhile, were well along their way when they happened to hear someone say that in the region to the rear of them something

15. Offerings of lamps and paper strips are made at Shinto shrines.

strange had happened and that a huge snake five arm-spans in length had appeared and was racing over the fields and hills in their direction. Hearing this, the monks thought, "This must surely be that woman of the house who, because we broke our promise, has become possessed by evil designs, turned into a poisonous snake, and is coming to pursue us!" They fled as fast as they could, seeking refuge in a temple called Dōjō-ji.

The monks of the temple, seeing the two monks, asked what they were running away from. They explained what had happened and begged for help. The temple monks gathered together to discuss what to do. They decided to lower the large bell that was hanging in the bell tower, instructing the young monk to hide inside the bell, after which they shut the temple gate. The old monk, along with the temple monks, hid elsewhere.

After a while, a huge snake arrived at the temple gate. Although the gate was closed, the snake climbed over it. Then it circled several times around the bell tower. Arriving at the door to the bell tower, which held the bell in which the young monk was hiding, it knocked at the door with its tail some hundred times until it finally smashed it down. The snake then entered the bell tower, wound itself around the bell, and with its tail pounded on the dragon's head knob from which the bell was suspended, continuing to do so for five or six hours.

Terrified though they were, the monks of the temple, wondering what was happening, opened the doors of the surrounding buildings and gathered around to look. They saw tears of blood streaming from the eyes of the poisonous snake. It lifted up its head, licked with its tongue, and then climbed down and hurried away in the direction from which it had come.

Gathering around, the temple monks saw that the huge bell, seared in the hot poisonous breath of the snake, was wreathed in flames. No one could even come near it. Eventually, however, they were able to pour water on it and cool the bell. When they raised it and looked for the monk who had been inside, they found that he had been consumed by the fire—not even a trace of his bones remained. All that was left of him was a little ash. The old monk who had accompanied him, seeing this, wept and lamented and then went on his way.

Some time later, a venerable old monk of Dōjō-ji had a dream. In it a huge snake, bigger than the one that had appeared earlier, confronted him and spoke to him in these words: "I am the monk who was hidden in the bell here. That evil woman turned into a poisonous snake, and in the end I was overpowered by the snake and forced to become her husband. I've been reborn in a vile and lowly form and undergo countless torments. I do not think I have sufficient strength to free myself from these ills, although when I was alive I abided by the teachings of the Lotus Sutra. But if I could beg you, holy man, to favor us with your vast kindness and virtue, I believe we could escape these sufferings. In particular I beg you, acting in a spirit of impartial pity and compassion, ritually pure as you are, to write out a copy of 'The Life Span' chapter of the Lotus Sutra.[16] Present it as an offering to us, the two snakes; free us from our torments. For without the power of the Lotus Sutra, how else can we escape?" With these words, the snake departed. Then the monk woke from his dream.

Thereafter, the old monk, thinking it over, was all at once moved by a spirit of piety. He copied "The Life Span" chapter in his own hand and, sacrificing what few possessions he had, called the other monks together and held a one-day religious gathering to make offerings to the two snakes and free them from their trials.

Later the old monk dreamed that a monk and a woman appeared to him. Both, wreathed in smiles and with a look of joy on their faces, arrived at Dōjō-ji and bowed to him in obeisance. "Because in a state of purity you have cultivated roots of goodness," they said, "we have both been able to quickly cast off our snake bodies and journey to a much finer realm. I, the woman, have been reborn in the Trayastrimsha Heaven, and I, the monk, have ascended to the Tushita Heaven."[17] When they had finished making this announcement, the two of them went their separate ways, climbing into the sky. Then the monk woke from his dream.

Thereafter, the old monk both rejoiced and sorrowed, and had ever greater esteem for the power and authority of the Lotus Sutra, boundless

16. "The Life Span of the Thus Come One" is chapter 16 of the Lotus Sutra and the core of its teachings, in which the Buddha reveals that he attained enlightenment in the far distant past and remains constantly in the world to relieve suffering and bring enlightenment.
17. The Trayastrimsha Heaven is the second of the six heavens in the world of desire, where beings have an extremely long life span. The Tushita Heaven is the fourth of the six heavens, where bodhisattvas are reborn just before they attain buddhahood.

in his admiration. What had happened was in fact a striking demonstration of the spiritual potency of the Lotus Sutra, a thing to be wondered at. That these two beings could start anew, casting off their serpent bodies and being reborn in the heavens, was due solely to the power of the Lotus. All who observed or heard of this were inspired to revere and have faith in the Lotus Sutra, to copy and recite it. And what the old monk did—that, too, was admirable. To have acted so must mean that in some previous existence he was a good teacher of the doctrine. And if we think of it, the love that that evil woman felt for the monk—that, too, must have been caused by some bond from a previous existence.

Be that as it may, we know from examples such as this how fearful are the evil impulses in a woman's heart. Therefore, the Buddha sternly warned us to keep women at a distance. Understand this and avoid them. Such, then, is the story that has been handed down.

How Kaya no Yoshifuji of Bitchū Province Became the Husband of a Fox and Was Saved by Kannon (16:17)

Long ago in Bitchū Province, the district of Kaya, the village of Ashimori, there was a man known as Kaya no Yoshifuji. He knew how to profit from money transactions and was very rich. By nature wild and profligate, he was much given to amorous adventures.

In the fall of the eighth year of Kampei [896], when his wife had gone to the capital and Yoshifuji was staying at home alone—a widower, as it were—he went out one evening for a stroll. All at once, he caught sight of a beautiful young woman. He had never seen her before, but, roused to feelings of passion and desire, he tried to approach her. When she looked as though she was about to slip away, Yoshifuji came closer, took hold of her arm, and said, "Who are you?"

Although the woman was attractively dressed, she replied, "I'm no one at all." She spoke in a charming manner. "Come to my house," said Yoshifuji. "That would not be proper!" she replied, and seemed to be on the point of fleeing. "Then where do you live?" asked Yoshifuji. "I'll go there with you." "It's right close by," she said, and began to walk. Yoshifuji, holding her arm, went with her.

In no time, they came to a handsomely built house that one could see was properly furnished inside. "Strange," thought Yoshifuji, "I don't remember there being such a place!" Inside the house were men and women of various ranks all bustling around and exclaiming, "The young mistress is back!" "She must be the daughter of the family!" thought Yoshifuji, and very much pleased, he proceeded to spend the night with her.

The next morning, someone who was evidently the master of the house appeared and said to Yoshifuji, "Some bond of fate must have brought you here. And now you must remain with us."

Treated in a highly welcoming manner, Yoshifuji fell completely in love with the woman, vowed to be true to her forever, and, waking or sleeping, remained always by her side. As for his own wife and children, he never gave them a thought.

In the meantime, as evening came on and Yoshifuji failed to return, the people of his household thought, "As usual—off on one of his secret escapades!" Night came and, to their annoyance, still no sign of him. "What madness! Have people go look for him!" Past midnight, but although they scoured the neighborhood, no trace of his whereabouts. They wondered if he had gone away, but none of his traveling clothes were missing, only an ordinary white robe. While they were racing around, the night came to an end, but nowhere they looked yielded a clue. Had he been a younger man, they might have thought he had a sudden change of heart and become a monk, but that would have been impossibly strange behavior for a person of his kind.

While all this excitement went on, Yoshifuji was passing the months and years in his new location. His wife became pregnant, and when the months had gone by, she gave easy birth to a son. Thus he grew more devoted than ever to her. So the months and years passed, all was contentment; all, it seemed, was as he wished it to be.

After Yoshifuji's disappearance, the people of his household continued their search for him but met with no success. Yoshifuji's elder brother, the district chief Toyonaka; his younger brothers, the village administrator Toyokage and Toyotsune, the assistant priest of the Kibitsuhigo shrine and temple; and Yoshifuji's son, Tadasada, were persons of wealth. All, distressed and saddened by his disappearance, thought, "We must search for his remains!" Joining together in religious vows, they decided to fashion an image of the eleven-faced Kannon.[18] Carving a piece of yew wood, they created an image that was the same height as Yoshifuji had been and then, bowing in obeisance before it, voiced this prayer: "Show us where his remains are." And from the day when Yoshifuji first disappeared, they had begun to recite the *nembutsu*[19] and chant sutras, hoping to aid him in his next existence.

Meanwhile, at the house where Yoshifuji was staying, a layman carrying a stick suddenly thrust his way in. When the head of the household and the other inhabitants saw him, they all fled in abject terror. The layman, poking Yoshifuji in the back with his stick, forced him to leave the house by way of a narrow passage.

It was the evening of the thirteenth day since Yoshifuji's disappearance. His people, missing him and grieving, said to one another, "What a peculiar way to disappear! And it was just about this time of evening!" At that moment, a strange black creature looking something like a monkey, its rear end in the air, crawled out from under the storehouse in front of them. "What's this!" they exclaimed, demanding an explanation. "It's me!" said a voice, and it was Yoshifuji's. Peculiar as it was, his son, Tadasada, recognized it as without doubt his father's voice. "What are you doing here?" said Tadasada, falling to the ground and pulling up the creature.

"Those times in the past when I was alone—a widower, as it were," said Yoshifuji, "I always used to long for a woman. Then suddenly I found I had to get married to a certain gentleman's daughter. And in the years since then, I've sired a son. He's a beautiful boy—day and night I fondle him, never letting him out of my arms. I call him Tarō, my firstborn, and you, Tadasada, I regard as my second son. That's because his mother is so dear to me."

18. The bodhisattva Avalokiteśvara is known in China as Guanyin and in Japan as Kannon, or Perceiver of the World's Sounds. Originally a male figure, he is often depicted in Chinese and Japanese art as a woman and is popularly referred to in English as the Goddess of Mercy. The eleven-faced Kannon is an image of Kannon with ten smaller heads placed above the main head.

19. The recitation of the words *Namu Amida Butsu*, or "Hail to Amida Buddha," is a petition to Amitābha, the central deity in Pure Land Buddhism.

Hearing this, Tadasada said, "And where is this precious son of yours?" "He's here," said Yoshifuji, and he pointed in the direction of the storehouse.

When Tadasada and the other members of the family heard this, they were dumbfounded. Looking at Yoshifuji, they saw that he had grown thin, as though suffering from an illness. Examining his clothes, they saw that they were the ones he had been wearing when he disappeared. And when they sent someone to examine the area under the storehouse, they found it teeming with foxes, all of which ran away. This was the place where Yoshifuji had been in hiding. Then it dawned on them: "Yoshifuji has been duped by one of these creatures and has become its husband. He's not in his right mind—that's why he talks like this."

Immediately, they summoned a high-ranking monk to conduct prayers, and called in an On'yōji master[20] to exorcise the evil. Yoshifuji was again and again bathed, and his hair washed, but he still did not look like his former self. Little by little, however, he returned to his right mind and felt great amazement and shame at what had happened.

Yoshifuji had remained under the storehouse for a period of thirteen days, and yet to him it seemed like thirteen years. When they took up the crossbeams under the storehouse, they found that there was no more than four or five inches of space under them. Yet Yoshifuji had viewed it as broad and lofty, and had gone in and out as though in a grand mansion. All this had been due to the uncanny powers exercised by the foxes. And as for the layman who came poking in with a stick—that was a manifestation of Kannon that had been fashioned for Yoshifuji's welfare.

Therefore, we know that people of our age should concentrate on devotions centering on Kannon. Yoshifuji suffered from no further illnesses and died at the age of sixty-one.

This incident was told to the Imperial Adviser Miyoshi no Kiyoyuki when he was governor of Bitchū.[21] Such, then, is the story that has been handed down.

20. An On'yōji (or Onmyōji) master is an expert in Chinese yin-yang divination and the avoidance of evil.
21. Miyoshi no Kiyoyuki (847–918), a Confucian scholar, served in the courts of five Heian-period emperors

How Ōe no Sadamoto, Governor of Mikawa, Became a Buddhist Monk (19:2)

Long ago, in the reign of Emperor En'yū [970–984], there was a man named Ōe no Sadamoto who was governor of Mikawa Province. He was the son of the Confucian scholar Ōe no Narimitsu, an Imperial Adviser, a Major Controller of the Left, and a Commissioner in the Ministry of Ceremony. He had a nature marked by pity and compassion and was a person of superior talent. After serving in the Chamberlain's Office, he was promoted to the post of governor of Mikawa.

In addition to the wife with whom he had lived from past times, Sadamoto was much taken with an attractive young woman of upright character. He found it all but impossible to dismiss her from his thoughts. His wife reacted with intense jealousy, and as a result the couple, forgetful of their matrimonial vows, abruptly parted. Sadamoto then made the young woman his wife, and she accompanied him when he went to his new post as governor of Mikawa.

After they reached Mikawa, the woman came down with a grave illness that caused her prolonged suffering. Sadamoto, grieved and distressed, did everything in his power to help, offering prayers for her recovery, but the illness showed no sign of mending. As the days went by, the woman's beautiful looks faded away. Observing this, Sadamoto's grief passed all description, but the woman's condition continued to worsen until she died.

Thereafter, plunged into bottomless despair, Sadamoto for a long time could not bear to carry out the funeral. He continued to cling to the corpse, but as the days passed and he kissed the woman's lips, a strange, foul-smelling odor emerged from them. Repelled in heart by this, he agreed to a funeral, weeping all the while. After that, Sadamoto came to look on the world as a hateful place, and his thoughts all at once began to turn to religion.

In the province to which he had been assigned, the local people carried out what was known as the Wind Festival.[22] At that time, Sadamoto observed how the people caught a wild boar and, while it was still alive, cut it up as an offering. "I must get out of this province at once!" he thought, and he became more determined than ever to enter religious life.

In addition to the boar, the people caught a pheasant and brought that also as a live offering. The governor said, "Well, now, are we going to eat the pheasant alive too? We might try to see how delicious it is that way." Hearing this, some of his underlings, not stopping to consider but hoping to ingratiate themselves with the governor, said, "That would be splendid! The flavor would be even better that way," and they urged him to proceed.

Those in the group who had some feeling about such matters thought to themselves, "What a barbarous way to do things!" But the others brought the pheasant and began to pluck its feathers while it was still alive. For a time, the bird fluttered its wings in alarm, but they pinned it down and went on plucking. Tears of blood began to flow from the bird's eyes as it batted its eyelids and looked from one in the group to another, so that some of them, unable to bear the sight, stopped what they were doing. Others, however, exclaimed, "Look—the bird is crying!" and, laughing and heartless, went on with their plucking.

When the plucking was done and the carving began, the blood gushed out in torrents under the blade. Again and again, they had to wipe the blade, until the bird, emitting an unbearably piteous cry, finally died. This done, they began to roast it over a fire. "You'd be surprised!" they said. "It tastes much better than roasting a bird that's already been dead!"

Sadamoto, watching all this intently and listening to what was said, burst out crying, huge tears rolling from his eyes, appalled that anyone could talk about how good something tastes at such a time. That very day, he left the provincial office and journeyed to the capital, resolved once and for all to enter religious life. Cutting off his topknot, he became a priest, taking the religious name Jakushō. The people of the time referred to him

---

22. The ceremony petitions the wind god to spare the region from wind damage.

as the lay monk of Mikawa.²³ He had observed these strange events of the Wind Festival in order to affirm beyond all doubt his determination to enter religious life.

Thereafter, Jakushō went from place to place in the capital, spreading the doctrine and soliciting contributions. Arriving at a certain house, he was invited to come in, shown to a seating mat, served a splendid meal, and urged to eat. The curtain to the inner apartments was then raised, and a woman dressed in fine clothes appeared. When Jakushō looked closely, he saw that it was none other than the wife from whom he had separated long ago.

"This beggar!" she said, as they stared at each other. "I always thought I'd see the day when you were begging for your food!" But Jakushō showed not the slightest sign of embarrassment. "You honor me greatly!" he said, and proceeded to eat the fine food that had been served him and then take his leave. His attitude was one of sincere gratitude. Because of his adherence to religious principles, though he was treated as some sort of pariah, he did not allow this to disturb him. This was most admirable.

Later, Jakushō decided that he wanted to journey to China to pay his respects at the outstanding holy places associated with the Buddhist faith. At the time he made this decision, he had a son, a monk named ——,²⁴ living on Mount Hiei.²⁵ In order to take his leave before setting off for China, Jakushō climbed Mount Hiei, visited the Konponchūdō, and paid his respects at the Hie Shrine. On his way back, he stopped at the lodge where his son, the monk ——, was living and knocked at the door. The door opened, and —— appeared on the veranda. It was the middle of the Seventh Month,²⁶ and the moon was shining brightly.

23. A lay monk (nyūdō), whose head is shaven, observes certain monastic precepts while continuing to live in society rather than in a temple.
24. There is a blank in the text wherever the monk's name would have appeared. Apparently, the compiler intended to fill in the blanks, but was not able to do so.
25. Mount Hiei, northeast of Kyoto, is the headquarters of the Tendai school and one of the most important centers of Japanese Buddhism. The Konponchūdō and the Hie Shrine, mentioned in the next sentence, are among the main sites of worship on the mountain.
26. The Seventh Month of the lunar calendar corresponds to August or September in the solar calendar.

Jakushō, addressing his son on the veranda, said, "I am determined to pay my respects to the holy sites of Buddhism, worthy as they are of veneration, and so I am setting out for China. It may be difficult for me to return from such a journey, and so tonight will perhaps be our last meeting. You must without fail remain on this mountain, continue your religious practice, and never be remiss in your studies." Jakushō shed tears as he spoke these words, and —— too wept endlessly.

When Jakushō started on his return to the capital, —— went as far as Great Peak to see him off. The moon was exceedingly bright, and dew bathed the surroundings in a white sheen. Autumn insects with their varied voices lent an air of sadness. Everything contrived to fill one with melancholy and wake sorrow in the heart. The son was about to accompany Jakushō down the mountain, but Jakushō said, "You must hurry back now!" With this, the son, weeping all the while, turned back, his figure fading from sight in the mist.

In time, Jakushō, having journeyed to China, paid his respects at the various holy places as he had planned. The emperor of the country received him in audience, treated him with the utmost respect, and gave ear to his teachings.

At that time, the emperor called together all the most outstanding religious figures of the realm, decorated a hall to receive them, had food suitable for monks prepared, and cordially invited them to help themselves. The emperor announced, "At today's religious feast, we won't be having any attendants to serve the food. So may I ask each of you to take the bowl that is placed in front of you, cause it to fly through the air, and in this way receive your portion of the food." His object in doing this was to put Jakushō to a test.

Following the emperor's instructions, each of the monks, beginning with the one seated in the place of honor, caused his bowl to fly through the air and in this way received his helping of the food. Jakushō, since he had entered the monastic order at a more recent date than the others, had been assigned to the lowest seat. When his turn came, he picked up his bowl and rose from his seat. But others in the group said, "Why are you doing that? Make your bowl fly through the air and get your fare that way!"

At that time, Jakushō, holding up his bowl, said, "To make one's bowl fly through the air requires a very special technique. One must learn the art before one can do so. But I have never studied that art. It is said that in Japan in ancient times there were a few people who performed this feat, but now in this latter age there is no one who can do so. Hence the art has been lost. How, then, could I possibly make my bowl fly through the air?"

"The reverend from Japan is too slow, too slow with his bowl!" said the others accusingly. Jakushō, greatly troubled in mind, exerted all his mental energy, saying to himself, "You Three Treasures of Japanese Buddhism, help me! If I cannot make my bowl fly through the air, it will mean extreme disgrace for the country of Japan!" With that, the bowl in front of Jakushō suddenly began to spin around and around like a top, sailing through the air even faster than the bowls of the other monks, and returned to him filled with his portion.

At that time, everyone, from the emperor down to the high ministers and the hundred officials, applauded Jakushō and paid him unlimited respect. And thereafter, the emperor was more heedful than ever of his doctrines.

Jakushō also made a pilgrimage to Mount Wutai.[27] There he performed various acts designed to bring religious benefit, such as having water heated to provide a bath for the community of monks. When the monks had gathered at that time to enjoy a communal meal, a very dirty-looking woman, carrying a child and accompanied by a dog, appeared in front of Jakushō. Because the woman was covered with unspeakably ugly sores, the others in the group, seeing her, were repulsed and tried to drive her away. But Jakushō, restraining them, gave the woman her helping of the food and prepared to send her off.

The woman said, "My body is covered with sores that are almost too much to endure. I've come so I can bathe in the water. Please let me receive a little benefit from the hot water!" The others, hearing this, drove her back, so she was forced to withdraw to a distance. Nevertheless, she managed to

---

27. Mount Wutai, a center of Buddhist activity in northeastern Shanxi Province, is noted in particular for the worship of Mañjuśri, the bodhisattva of wisdom.

steal into the bathhouse, where, holding the child and accompanied by the dog, she splashed about in the hot water.

When the others heard what she was doing, they cried, "Drive her out!" But when they looked in the bathhouse, she had disappeared as though by magic. They were startled and mystified by this, but when they emerged from the bathhouse and looked around, they saw a purple cloud gleaming and rising beyond the eaves. "It must have been Mañjuśri, who changed into the shape of a woman and appeared here!" they exclaimed. Weeping tears of regret, they bowed to the ground in obeisance, but by that time it was too late.

These last events took place when Jakushō was accompanied by his disciple, the monk Nengu. When Nengu returned to Japan, he relayed an account of them.[28] He told how Jakushō had won over the emperor of China to his teachings, and how the latter had bestowed on him the title Great Teacher and the religious name Entsū.[29]

Thus we learn how a man, impelled by certain causes, entered religious life and, traveling to a foreign country, was received with honor there. Such, then, is the story that has been handed down.

How a Palace Guard of the Takiguchi Unit Went to Collect Gold During the Reign of Emperor Yōzei (20:10)

Long ago in the reign of Emperor Yōzei,[30] a man named Michinori of the Takiguchi unit of the Palace Guard was sent to the region of Michinoku to collect some gold. While he was carrying out this mission, he put up for the night at a place called —— in Shinano Province. It was the house of

28. Nengu returned to Japan in 1013. Some texts identify Nengu as a Chinese monk, but, as the text indicates here, he was originally from Japan.
29. The *History of the Song* (Ch. *Song shi*, Jp. *Sōshi*, 1346) records that Jakushō went to China in 1004 and was honored with the name Great Teacher Yuantong or Entsū. Because he could not speak Chinese, he communicated with the emperor "by brush"—that is, in writing. He died in China in 1034.
30. Yōzei (r. 877–884) was deposed at age eighteen because of signs of mental instability.

an official of the local government, where he was cordially received. After he had dined and all his other needs had been attended to, his host and his attendants withdrew to another house.

Michinori, on a journey and finding himself unable to sleep, got up and began to wander about, when he happened to glimpse the wife of the official asleep in an adjoining room. She was surrounded by screens and curtains, the tatami were clean and neat, and a two-tiered offertory was placed conveniently by. A faint scent hung in the air, lending a subtle perfume.

Given the rural setting, Michinori was surprised at this. Looking more closely, he could see a woman of twenty or more lying there gracefully, her hair carefully arranged, her forehead clear, and in the rest of her nothing whatsoever out of place. As Michinori gazed at her, he felt that he could never pass up such a sight. And as there was no one around, there was no one to stop him as he softly drew aside the sliding door and entered.

There was no one to say, "Who's there?" A light had been placed behind the curtain but shone brightly. Although he could not help feeling guilty before the figure of the wife of the provincial official, sound asleep before him, looking at her, he felt a compelling urge to move forward.

He got in beside the figure in the bed, though not without some hesitation. Her mouth was open, and her sleeping face seemed more alluring the nearer he came to it. Michinori was beside himself with delight.

It was around the tenth day of the Ninth Month, and she was lightly clothed, wearing only a single robe of pale lavender twill and dark red trousers, from which exuded a delightful fragrance. Michinori quickly doffed his garments and moved into her arms. For a while, he worked his way closer and closer, taking no notice of her signs of resistance. But all at once he felt an itching sensation in his *mara*.[31] He began to fumble around for it, but all he came on was hair. His *mara* had disappeared!

In alarm and wonder, he searched here and there, but he could find nothing but hair like that on a head. There was no trace of it! In his terror, he forgot all about the charms of the woman. The woman, observing the alarm and distress of the man, gave a faint laugh.

---

31. A Sanskrit word meaning "devil," *mara* entered Japanese by way of Buddhism and was used as a term for "penis."

Michinori, less and less inclined to proceed, thinking it all strange, stealthily rose and returned to his original sleeping place, all thought of venturing abroad abandoned. But then a thought occurred to him, and he called to his attendant whom he was accustomed to working with. Saying nothing of what had just happened, he mentioned casually, "There's a beautiful woman in there. I've already visited her—so it must be your turn now."

The attendant, delighted, hurried off. After a while, he came back, with a peculiar expression on his face. "So he must have met the same fate," thought Michinori, and he called to another attendant and sent him off. This one, too, came back, gazing up at the sky with a look of profound dissatisfaction. It went on like this, until he had sent seven or eight attendants, all of whom came back with the same troubled expression on their faces.

While these strange happenings were being repeated over and over, the night came to an end. As Michinori thought over its events, he could not help being delighted by the gracious welcome he had received from his host. But at the same time, there were those extremely strange and unsettling events that followed. He decided to put the whole thing out of his mind, and as the night ended, he and his party quickly got under way.

They had not gone more than seven or eight *chō*[32] when they heard someone calling. Turning to look, they saw a horse and rider coming their way. When he arrived, he turned out to be an attendant from the previous evening, who presented something wrapped in white paper. "What's this?" asked Michinori, reining in his horse.

"This," said the man, "is something the provincial official said to present to you. He wondered why you went off without them. As usual, we made preparations for breakfast, but you were in a hurry and went off without them, so we gathered them up and respectfully present them." Wondering what was in the package, he opened it—to find nine *mara*, wrapped as though they were *matsutake* mushrooms.

Startled, he called the others to gather around. Eight attendants, all wondering what was in the package, came to see. There were nine *mara*, one for

---

32. A *chō*, here a unit of length, is about 360 feet.

each of the group who had lost them. The messenger, having handed them over, wheeled his horse around and made off. At that time, each of the attendants admitted, "Yes—it happened to me, too!" But when they looked, they discovered that their *mara* were in their usual place. With this, they hurried on their way to Michinoku Province, to which they had been sent to collect a shipment of gold. On their way back, they put up at the same house of the provincial official of Shinano where they had stayed before.

The official, delighted at all the presents of horses, silks, and other items they had brought him, exclaimed, "What's all this for?" Michinori, drawing close to him, said, "It is a matter of great shame to tell you this, but the time I stayed here before, a most peculiar thing happened. I don't understand it, and so, shameful as it is, I want to ask you about it."

The provincial official, having received a great many gifts, spoke out without hiding anything. "When I was young, I served in one of the remoter districts of this province, under an old official who had a young wife. I paid a call on her, lost my *mara*, and thought it very strange. But I managed to get close to the old man and learned the secret. If you want to learn it, well, you've brought me all these presents. So sometime when you are free, I'll teach it to you."

Michinori promised that that would be satisfactory, and hurried on his way to the capital with the gold. When he had completed his mission, he returned to Shinano.

He brought with him appropriate gifts that, when presented, pleased the provincial official. "I'll teach you the best I can," he said. "But this technique is not easily learned. It takes seven days of intense effort, every day bathing in water. Tomorrow you will begin the process!"

Accordingly, Michinori began the following day, each day cleansing himself by bathing in water. When the seven days came to an end, the provincial official and Michinori, just the two of them, went deep into the mountains, to a place where a large river flowed by. "You must for a long time abandon faith in the Three Treasures," warned the provincial official, and in various other ways he led him in making unspeakably sinful declarations.

That done, the official said, "Now we must go into the water. Whatever thing comes out of it, be it god or devil, you must embrace it!" With this, the official entered the water.

After a while, the sky over the water grew dark, thunder rolled, wind blew, and rain began to fall, swelling the river. Soon a snake's head appeared, rising from the water, its eyes flashing like sparks from a metal bowl. Its belly was red and its back was dark blue, sparkling as though coated with a blue sheen. "Clasp what has come flowing down" came the order, but Michinori was so frightened that he hid in a clump of grass.

After a moment, the provincial official appeared. "Well, did you take hold of it?" he asked. "No, I didn't—I was too frightened!" Michinori replied. "Oh, what a shame!" he exclaimed. "However, this technique is very difficult to acquire. But you can try again," he said, and Michinori entered the water again.

After a while, a boar appeared, some four *shaku*[33] in length, with tusks stretching out, chomping on stones, fire flying from it, its fur standing on end. It was a most terrifying sight, but Michinori thought, "It's now or never!" and moved forward and embraced it—to find himself embracing an old rotten log three *shaku* long.

At that moment, he was overcome by anger and regret. "The first one, too, was probably nothing more than this!" he thought. "Why didn't I embrace it?"

"What happened?" asked the provincial official, stepping forward.

"I embraced it," replied Michinori.

"That other technique—the one having to do with losing your *mara*—you didn't get that. But you seem to have gotten some other inferior technique. In that case, I'll explain it to you," said the official. He told him what it was and then sent him on his way. But Michinori always regretted that he'd never learned the technique that pertained to a lost *mara*.

After returning to the capital, Michinori entered the service of the emperor. In the office of the Takiguchi unit of the Palace Guard, he was involved in the contention over the burning of the shoes, during which all the officials quarreled with one another like little children. And then there was the case of the old straw shoes that transformed into a three-*shaku* carp on the serving tray, flapping around as though still alive.

33. A *shaku* is a little less than one foot.

Because of reports of these happenings, Emperor Yōzei summoned Michinori to the Black Door imperial residence, where he was employed. After that, he was chosen from his post at the side bar and allowed to take part in the festival at the Kamo Shrine.

There were persons of the time who disapproved of these moves. Hence the rumors that the emperor himself had for long been practicing arts that differed from those of the Three Treasures. But those who said so were slanderers. These stories were put about by low and worthless members of society, a very serious crime. It is perhaps because of these slanders that rumors have arisen of the emperor's madness.

As for these rumors of the worship of devils and the disparagement of the Three Treasures: It is difficult to be born a human being, and difficult to encounter a time when Buddhist teachings are in effect. Therefore, to be fortunate enough to be born a human being and at a time when the Buddhist teachings prevail, and yet to cast aside Buddhism and turn one's attention to the world of devils is like going to a mountain of treasures and returning empty-handed, like embracing a stone and plunging into a deep pool, thereby putting an end to one's life. Hence it is said that one should never follow such ways!

SECULAR TALES OF JAPAN

The stories in book 25, which focus on warriors, particularly the Taira and Minamoto clans during the Heian period, are arranged in roughly chronological order, foreshadowing medieval *gunki-mono* (warrior tales). The story "How a Child of Fujiwara no Chikakatsu, Having Been Taken Hostage by a Thief, Was Released Through Words Spoken by Yorinobu" (25:11) belongs to a series (25:9–11) that reveals the wisdom of the military lord Minamoto no Yorinobu. The next story, "How Minamoto no Yorinobu's Son Yoriyoshi Shot Down a Horse Thief" (25:12), in addition to illustrating the ideal relationship between father and son, demonstrates one of the indispensable skills of the new class of warriors: communicating without words.

Book 26, tales of *shukuhō* (retribution), gathers stories about strange and extraordinary events from a wide variety of sources, including the life of commoners in the provinces, and attributes the miraculous to karmic acts in a previous life. Book 27, tales of "ghosts or spirits" (*reikon*), includes stories about supernatural beings—such as demons, foxes, wild boars, and mountain deities—and explores the interaction between the human and supernatural worlds. The volume has been considered the first collection of Japanese *kaidan* (ghost stories), a popular genre in the Edo period (1600–1867). Two examples are "How the Demon at Agi Bridge in Ōmi Province Ate Somebody" (27:13), which describes the trickery employed by demons and suggests the extent to which commoners of the time feared ghosts, demons, and strange monsters, and "How Ki no Tōsuke of Mino Province Met Female Spirits and Died" (27:21).

Book 28 consists of humorous tales, which encompass characters from every level of society and take place both inside and outside the capital. Two of these *setsuwa* are "How a Group of Nuns Went into the Mountains, Ate Some Mushrooms, and Danced" (28:28) and "How Fujiwara no Nobutada, Governor of Shinano, Took a Tumble at Misaka" (28:38). The latter, which is noted for its depiction of the *zuryō* (provincial governor) class, became so famous that it coined a saying (*kotowaza*): "Wherever the provincial governor stumbles, he snatches a handful of dirt." The *setsuwa* reveals the nature of the nobility who went from the capital to the provinces to try to gather as much wealth for themselves as possible. The provincial governor is the object of laughter, detestation as well as awe.

Book 29, tales of "evil acts" (*akugyō*), covers a wide variety of heinous deeds, particularly robbery and murder. Two examples are "How a Thief Climbed to the Upper Story of Rashōmon Gate and Came on a Corpse" (29:18) and "How a Man Was Traveling with His Wife to Tanba and Got Tied Up at Ōeyama" (29:23), which have to do with a thief and a rapist, respectively. Both stories were used by the novelist Akutagawa Ryūnosuke (1892–1927) as the basis for his short story "Rashōmon" and then by the film director Kurosawa Akira (1910–1998) in a film by the same name. The last part of book 29 contains stories about animals (such as tiger, dog, monkey, and hawk), which appear in this section because one of the "three evil paths" (*sanakudō*) in the Buddhist cosmology, along with hell and the "sphere of hungry ghosts," was the "sphere of beasts" (*chikushōdō*), while some of the stories are about the sin of killing animals.

Book 30 concentrates on tales about *waka* (classical poetry), some of which are drawn from *Toshiyori's Poetic Essentials* (*Toshiyori zuinō*, ca. 1115), a poetry treatise by the noted *waka* poet Minamoto no Toshiyori (1055?–1129) that contains numerous anecdotes about *waka*. Many of these stories overlap with those in *The Tales of Yamato* (*Yamato monogatari*, ca. 951), a poem-tale (*uta-monogatari*) collection of the Heian period. Unlike most *setsuwa*, these center on *waka* and, in this sense, bear resemblances to the *uta-monogatari* genre. The story "How a Poor Man Left His Wife and She Became the Wife of the Governor of Settsu" (30:5), which appears in a different form in *Yamato monogatari* (148), was recast by the novelist Tanizaki Jun'ichirō (1886–1965) as the novella *Reed Cutter* (*Ashikari*). Like a number of other stories in this book, this *setsuwa* deals with love and separation and shows the influence of the court tale tradition, but it differs in its concentration on the lowly position of the man.

How a Child of Fujiwara no Chikakatsu, Having Been Taken Hostage by a Thief, Was Released Through Words Spoken by Yorinobu (25:11)

Long ago, when Minamoto no Yorinobu, Lord of Kawachi, was acting as Lord of Kamitsuke and had lands in that region,[34] he had a samurai named Hyō-no-jō Fujiwara no Chikakatsu, who had a son in the care of a nursemaid. He was a valiant warrior and shared with Yorinobu the management of the fief.

A thief broke into the house where Chikakatsu was staying, and though he was apprehended and bound hand and foot, he somehow managed to escape from his bonds, perhaps because proper precautions had not been taken. Chikakatsu's son was only five or six at the time, a very likable child,

---

34. Historical records confirm Minamoto no Yorinobu in this position in the year 999.

but as he was running away, he was seized as a hostage by the thief, who thrust him into a storeroom, made him lie down under his legs, drew his sword, and held it against the boy's abdomen.

At that time, his father, Chikakatsu, was in the office, when a man came running in and reported that the boy had been taken hostage by the thief. Chikakatsu, alarmed, rushed to the scene, only to find that the thief had in fact forced the boy into a storeroom and held his sword pressed against the boy's abdomen. Looking at them, his eyes went dim with fear, but there was nothing he could do. Although he would like to have said, "Just get him out of this!" as he looked at the huge sword pressing even now against the boy's abdomen, all he could say was, "Don't go near them! If you do, he'll kill him!" He knew that if the thief actually killed the boy, they could chop his bones into a hundred or a thousand pieces and it would make no difference. His retainers agreed. "Look out—don't go near them! Watch them from a distance!" they said, and went to report to Lord Yorinobu on what had happened.

Before long, the tension and excitement of what had happened had spread to the place where Yorinobu, the one in command, was located. "What is going on here?" he demanded in alarm. Chikakatsu, weeping, replied, "It is just that my son, who was all alone at the time, has been taken hostage by a thief!"

Yorinobu laughed. "I understand how you feel," he said, "but is this a cause for weeping? Whether you're dealing with a god or a devil, you have to face the situation. Rather than weeping for your son, I'd say better to laugh at the affair! One little boy gets put to death—what of that? That's what soldiers do. To think of themselves or their wives and family—that is to betray themselves! They stand fearless—no thought of self, no thought of family. And I stand with them!" So saying, he put on his sword and pushed Chikakatsu aside.

The thief, seeing that the Lord was present, did not bluster as he had when Chikakatsu first observed him, but behaved in a rather subdued manner, though he pressed closer and closer with his sword, as if to say, "One more from you, and you're done for!" Meanwhile, the child cried piteously.

The Lord, observing them, said, "You there—are you holding this child a hostage so you can preserve your life? Or do you just intend to kill him? You fool—say once and for all what you're up to!"

The thief, speaking in an apologetic manner, replied, "What business would I have killing a child? I only seized him because I thought I could preserve my life that way."

"Then put your sword aside!" said the Lord. "That's what I'm telling you—and you can't do other than obey! I'm not here to watch any killing. And what I say naturally goes. So put it aside, you fool!"

The thief seemed to ponder this for a moment. "Why not obey your illustrious command? I put my sword aside," he said, and he threw it away. The child leaped up, happy to make his escape, and the thief quickly followed him.

The Lord, after withdrawing a little, addressed his retainers and said, "Call that fellow over here!" The retainers seized the thief by the collar of his robe and dragged him into the courtyard, where they put him down. Chikakatsu demanded that he be put to death. But the Lord said, "This fool, pitiful as he is, should be forgiven for taking a hostage. Because he was poor, he turned to thieving, and he took the boy hostage because he thought it would spare him his life. There's nothing to hate about that! Furthermore, when I said spare the child, he listened and spared the child. Although he is a thief, he understands things. Let him go!"

"Is there anything you need? Speak up!" When the Lord asked him this, the thief only stood there weeping.

"Get some food for this fellow!" said the Lord. "He may do something bad again and end up killing somebody. And go in the stables and fetch one of the ordinary horses—one of the stronger ones—and fit it with one of the inferior saddles," he said. He also had him fitted with an inferior type of bow and quiver. When all these items had been supplied and he was fitted with a quiver and mounted on his horse, he was given a ten-day supply of rations, wrapped in a sack and fastened to his waist. "Now you're ready to go!" said the Lord, and with these words he galloped off.

The thief is believed to have undergone an awakening at these words of Yorinobu's and to have given up taking hostages. Thus we see that Yorinobu understood all the various needs of a warrior.

As for the boy who was taken hostage, later, when he grew up, he went to Mount Mitake, entered the priesthood, and eventually became an *ajari*.[35] His name is said to have been Myōshu.

How Minamoto no Yorinobu's Son Yoriyoshi Shot Down a Horse Thief (25:12)

Long ago there was a warrior named Lord Minamoto no Yorinobu,[36] the former governor of Kawachi Province. Having heard of a very fine horse in the eastern region, this Minamoto no Yorinobu sent someone to ask for the horse. The owner found it difficult to refuse, and so he allowed the horse to be taken to the capital.

Along the way, a horse thief caught sight of the animal and felt an intense desire to possess it. "I must arrange to steal it," he thought, and, keeping out of sight, he followed the horse. But the band of warriors who were escorting the horse never once let down their guard, and so the thief had no chance to steal it while they were on the road. Thus he followed the party until they reached the capital. Once in the capital, the horse was put away in the stables belonging to Minamoto no Yorinobu.

Meanwhile, someone reported to Yorinobu's son Yoriyoshi, "Today your father acquired a very fine horse from the eastern region." Yoriyoshi said to himself, "The horse will probably end up in the hands of somebody of no importance just because the person asked for it. Before that happens, I'd better take a look at it myself. If it's a really fine animal, I'll ask my father to give it to me!" With that thought in mind, he went to his father's house.

A very heavy rain was falling, but Yoriyoshi was so eager to see the horse that he did not allow that to deter him. When he arrived around nightfall, his father said, "Why has it been such a long time since I've seen you?" And

35. *Ajari* was a high post in the priesthood of the Shingon school, which held power at Mount Mitake.
36. Both Yorinobu (968–1048) and Yoriyoshi (995–1082) were distinguished military figures who played an important role in putting down revolts against the government.

Minamoto no Yorinobu's son Yoriyoshi takes aim at the horse thief, who is crossing the river in the dark, while his father gives orders. (From an Edo-period wood-block edition of *Konjaku monogatari shū*, with the permission of Komine Kazuaki)

then he said, "Ah—I see. You've heard that I've acquired this horse. And you've come because you thought you'd ask for it."

Then, before Yoriyoshi knew quite how to respond to this, his father said, "They tell me the horse from the eastern region has arrived, but I haven't had a look at it yet. The person who sent it assures me it's a fine animal. It's already dark now, so we can't look at it tonight. We'll wait until tomorrow, and if it suits you, you can take it with you at once."

Yoriyoshi, spoken to in this manner before he had even asked for the horse, thought to himself, "Fine!" "In that case," he said, "I'll stay here tonight to help guard things, and we'll have a look at the horse tomorrow." Accordingly, he prepared to spend the night.

As the evening wore on, the two men chatted together. Then, when it grew late, the father retired to his room and went to bed, while Yoriyoshi lay down nearby to nap and act as a guard.

Meanwhile, the sound of the falling rain continued without stop. Around the middle of the night, the horse thief, taking advantage of the rain, stole in and made off with the horse. From the direction of the stables a voice was heard calling out, "That horse they brought here last evening— a thief has stolen it and gotten away!"

Yorinobu was just barely able to catch the words. Not stopping to ask his son Yoriyoshi, who was still asleep, whether he had heard the cry, he leaped up and threw on his clothes. Tucking in the bottom of his robe and slinging a quiver and arrows over his shoulder, he ran to the stables. There he led out another horse, tossed a plain saddle on it, and, mounted on this, raced off in pursuit toward Barrier Hill.[37] "The thief," Yorinobu thought to himself, "came from the east. Seeing what a fine horse it was, he hoped to steal it, but he couldn't do so along the way. And now, coming to the capital and taking advantage of the rain, he's made off with it!" This thought in mind, he pressed on his way.

But Yoriyoshi, too, had heard the cry. His thoughts following the same pattern as those of his father, he did not stop to speak to Yorinobu. Since he had not taken off his regular clothes but had slept in them, he got up and,

---

37. Barrier Hill is the site of the barrier gate in Yamashina, east of Kyoto, on the main road leading to eastern Japan. Travelers on the road were stopped at the gate for questioning.

dressed as he was, slung a quiver over his shoulder and, as his father had done, made for the stables. ———,[38] rode off alone in the direction of Barrier Hill in pursuit of the thief.

Yorinobu thought, "My son will surely follow in pursuit." And Yoriyoshi thought, "My father must have gone ahead of me in pursuit." Each galloping along so as not to fall behind, one by one they crossed the bed of the Kamo River.[39] By this time, the rain had let up and the sky was clear. Galloping faster than ever in pursuit, they reached Barrier Hill.

The thief, meanwhile, mounted on the stolen horse, thought, "Now I can make my escape!" But in the area around Barrier Hill, there was a good deal of water,[40] and he had to pick his way along slowly, splash-splashing through the water as he went.

When Yorinobu heard this, it was as though he had been given exact instructions where to shoot. And although it was pitch dark, and he didn't know whether his son was beside him or not, he said, "Now—shoot there!" Before he had even finished speaking, the twang of a bow rang out. And then, just as a sound told him there had been a hit, he could hear a horse galloping, its stirrups making a clattering noise that indicated it was riderless.

Again Yorinobu spoke up. "The thief's been hit, and he's fallen off! Quick!" he shouted. "Go after the horse and bring it back!" Then, without waiting to see if anyone retrieved the horse, he started back for the capital. Yoriyoshi went after the horse and retrieved it.

When Yorinobu's underlings got word of what had happened, one or two of them came out on the road to join Yoriyoshi and Yorinobu. By the time they returned to their home in the capital, they made up a party of twenty or thirty men.

After Yorinobu got home, he did not say a word about who had done this or who had done that but, since it was still night, went back to bed as he had been before. Yoriyoshi, too, after he had turned over the stolen horse to the stable attendants, went back to bed.

---

38. There is a lacuna in the original text.
39. The Kamo is the shallow river that marks the eastern boundary of the capital.
40. The ground was wet presumably because of the heavy rain that had fallen.

When the night was over, Yorinobu got up and called to his son. He did not say anything about how it was lucky that the horse hadn't been stolen or that somebody had been a good shot. Instead he said, "Bring the horse here." When the horse had been brought out, Yoriyoshi could see just how fine it was and said, "Well, then, I'll take it!" and proceeded to make the horse his own. At some point during the night, however, the horse had been fitted with a splendid saddle. This, we may suppose, was Yoriyoshi's reward for having shot a thief in the night.

How strange are their ways! But this, it would seem, is how the warriors do things. This is the story that has been handed down.

How the Demon at Agi Bridge in Ōmi Province Ate Somebody (27:13)

Long ago, when a man named —— was governor of Ōmi Province,[41] there were several young men in the governor's office who were noted for their high spirits. Years after, people still speak of how they played *go* or *suguroku*,[42] went off on a thousand adventures, or ate and drank together. Or the time one of them said, "In this province we have a bridge called the Agi Bridge.[43] In the old days people used it, but nowadays for some reason no one goes over it anymore." One of them started it, but the others took it up, chattering enthusiastically. Then the bravest of them spoke up, noting that in fact no one used the Agi Bridge. "But I'll go over it! Whatever fearful demon there may be, I'll go over it riding on the fleetest horse in headquarters!"

At that, all the others voiced hearty approval. "Splendid!" they shouted. "Go to it! That's the shortest way, but everyone seems to be taking the long way, true or not. Look at the spirit he has!" they cried encouragingly.

41. Ōmi Province is roughly equivalent to present-day Shiga Prefecture, in which Lake Biwa is located.
42. *Go* and *suguroku* (more commonly, *sugoroku*) are board games, the latter played with dice. They are often used for gambling.
43. Agi apparently is an old name for the part of the Hino River that runs into the western side of Lake Biwa.

The young man races across Agi Bridge on a horse with the demon in pursuit. (From an Edo-period wood-block edition of *Konjaku monogatari shū*, with the permission of Komine Kazuaki)

While all this excitement was going on, the governor, hearing of it, said, "What's this fuss about?" When they gathered around and told him, he replied, "What a stupid thing for him to do! But as far as the horse goes, he can take it any time." The young man replied, "It was a crazy idea, just a whim. I'm sorry." But those opposing his quitting cried, "What nonsense! He's lost his nerve!" and urged him to go on.

"Crossing the bridge is easy enough," said the young man. "But it looks as though I'm just trying to get a horse." "Hurry up—it's getting late!" exclaimed the others. They put an easier saddle on the horse and then were ready. The young man had doubts, but it was he who had proposed the idea. The rear end of the horse was slathered with oil, the ropes holding the saddle were tightened, the whip was fitted to his hand with a ring, and the equipage was made as light as possible. He mounted the horse.

As the horse drew near the approach to the bridge, the young man felt fear gripping his heart, but he knew that it was too late to turn back. He noted with misgiving that the sun was nearing the line of mountains. Moreover, the spot was deserted, far from any village, with no sign of smoke rising from a house. Full of apprehension, he raced along toward the middle of the bridge when, far in the distance, he saw a figure.

That must be the demon, he thought, as he eyed it nervously. It wore a light-colored robe, a dark singlet, and red trousers. It covered its mouth and looked around in an indescribably pathetic manner. It was a woman. Her gaze conveyed a look of grief, as though, through no fault of her own, she had been abandoned. She was hanging onto the tall rail of the bridge, but when the young man looked at her, she assumed a look bashful but delighted.

At the sight of her, the young man was about to forget everything and invite her to come up and ride beside him, or perhaps to dismount. But he told himself, "There's no woman in a place like this—this is a demon!" and, shutting his eyes, he sped past her.

The woman had expected to be spoken to, but when he rushed by without a word, she cried, "Ah!—that gentleman—he just passes me by. In a place like this, and he goes off without stopping! At least take me to a village!" But it was no use. The man, frightened out of his wits, whipped up the horse and flew past her, leaving her cries of "Heartless!" echoing all around.

"Just as I thought," said the man to himself, and he began intoning "Kannon, save me!"[44] and whipping his horse to greater speed. The demon, running after, tried again and again to get a grip on the horse, but because of the oil spread on it, its hands kept slipping away.

As the man turned to look back, he could see the demon's face, vermillion in color and round like a sitting mat, and its single eye. It had three hands, with claws like knives five inches long. Its body was bluish-green in color, and its eye was amber. Its hair was in a tangle, like a bramble bush, and just looking at it turned one's heart cold, an unspeakable horror. But because he kept praying to Kannon as he raced along, the young man was able to reach safety in a place where other humans were about. At that time, the demon said, "Very well—but sometime we'll meet again!" and with that vanished from sight.

The young man, groaning, feeling not himself at all, made his way back to the provincial headquarters in the gathering dusk. "What happened?" asked the others. But he was so faint from fear that he could not answer. As the others gathered around to reassure him, he calmed down a little.

The governor too, worried, asked what had happened, and he replied with a full account. "It was stupid to begin with—and you almost lost your life!" declared the governor as he took charge of the horse. The young man, however, returned to his family with an air of triumph and, addressing his wife and family and the servants, told them all the fearful things that had happened.

From that time on, however, the family began to experience various strange occurrences. Consulting an On'yōji, or yin-yang master, about this, they were advised from that day on to exercise grave caution. Beginning that day, they shut their gate tight and observed utmost care.

The man had a younger brother, his only sibling, who was employed in the office of Michinoku Province. He, accompanied by their mother, was journeying to Ōmi Province and happened to arrive just when the family

---

44. Kannon, the bodhisattva known in English as the Goddess of Mercy, has vowed to aid those in trouble.

went into seclusion. When he knocked at the gate, he was told, "We are in strict seclusion. Please come another day. Meanwhile, you can put up somewhere else."

The younger brother said, "That's absurd! It's getting late, and even if I put up somewhere else, what about the things I've brought? In case the day was inauspicious, I planned it so I would arrive on a good day. And this elderly person with me, I'm afraid, has succumbed. So I have to announce that to you, too." The people in the house were greatly distressed at the news of the elderly parent, but they replied warily, "We are in strict seclusion." "Just quickly open the door!" was the tearful reply.

The older brother was in the parlor preparing to eat, but came to the door and, weeping copiously, spoke with the visitor. The younger brother in his black mourning garments was weeping, and the older brother was weeping, too. The wife of the latter, hiding behind the curtain, hearing the sound of weeping, wondered what was going on.

Suddenly the brothers rushed into each other's arms, making a great commotion. The wife, startled, cried out, "What's happening?" The older brother, holding the younger one down, shouted, "Quick—bring me the sword that's under the pillow!" "Heavens—are you crazy?" said his wife. "What's going on?" When she failed to bring it, he cried, "Just bring it! I'm going to kill him!"

But the younger brother, managing to get on top, held down his older brother, bit off his head, and—dancing around with it, looking in the direction of the wife, and holding it up—exclaimed, "What joy!" His face showed the triumph he felt at having avenged the "incident at the bridge." Then he vanished.

With that, the wife and all the other members of the household broke into tears, but there was nothing they could do about it.

A woman's wisdom is not worth counting on. They had lots of goods, horses, and so on when they looked, but they were no more than bare bones. "Anyone who would take part in a stupid contest like that is an utter fool!" All the people who heard what had happened blamed the man.

After that, there were various stories, and it appears that the demons were bested, as they are no longer heard of anymore.

How Ki no Tōsuke of Mino Province Met Female Spirits and Died (27:21)

Long ago, there was a man named Fujiwara no Takanori, a former official of Nagato. When he was serving as temporary governor of Shimōsa Province, he was assigned by the *kanpaku*[45] to oversee the affairs of the country estate of Namatsu in Mino Province. And attached to that estate was a man named Ki no Tōsuke.

Among the various people on the estate, Takanori took particular notice of this Ki no Tōsuke. Tōsuke was summoned to the capital for extended service in the Higashi no Sanjō Palace. His period of service in the capital having ended, he had been dismissed and was on his way home to Mino and was crossing the Seta Bridge.[46]

As he was doing so, he noted a woman standing and holding up the hem of her robe. Passing by on his horse, he thought this a little peculiar. "Where are you going, may I ask?" said the woman. "I'm going to Mino," replied Tōsuke, dismounting from his horse. "I have a favor to ask," she said. "I wonder if you would oblige me?" "I would be delighted," he replied.

"Ah, how happy you make me!" she exclaimed. Then, pulling a small box from the breast of her robe and unwrapping the piece of silk around it, she said, "If you could take this to the village of Morokoshi in the district of Kataagata, the place by the bridge where they store the produce. At the west end of the bridge, there will be a woman waiting. Please give this to her."

Tōsuke thought this rather strange, but he replied, "I will be happy to comply." Noting the woman's appearance, as though she were fearful that he would refuse, he found it difficult to deny her request. Accepting the box, he said, "This woman waiting by the bridge—who is she? Where does

---

45. The *kanpaku* (regent) in the government at the time was Fujiwara no Yoritori, who served as *kanpaku* from 1020 to 1067.

46. The bridge is at Ōtsu over the Seta River, which runs out of the southern end of Lake Biwa.

she live? If she's not there, how will I find her? And who should I say sent the box?"

The woman replied, "Just go to the foot of the bridge. She will be waiting to receive it. There's no mistake—she will be there. But for heaven's sake, do not ever try to open the box!" As she said this, Tōsuke had the feeling that the others in his party did not see him standing there and talking to her; they only saw that he had gotten off his horse and was standing there, and they wondered what he was doing. After Tōsuke had accepted the box, the woman went on her way.

Tōsuke, having remounted his horse, journeyed on to Mino. But when he reached the approach to the bridge at Morokoshi, he forgot all about what he was supposed to do there and failed to deliver the box. Only when he reached home did he remember. "Well, I'll have to look for the woman another time and hand it over then," he thought to himself as he put it away in what he thought was a safe place.

Tōsuke's wife was of a very jealous nature, and she happened to come across the box by accident. "He must have bought it and brought it from Kyoto, intending to give it to some woman!" she thought. "And he's hidden it from me here!" When Tōsuke had gone out, his wife got out the box and opened it. In it, she found several human eyes that had been gouged out and a number of penises with a little of the hair attached.

When the wife saw these things, she was greatly startled and frightened. As soon as Tōsuke returned, with much misgiving she called him to look at them. "She warned me not to open the box!" he exclaimed. "Now you've done it!"

Quickly he wrapped the things up again the way they had been and, as the woman had told him, took the box to the foot of the bridge. There was a woman waiting there, as he had been told there would be. When Tōsuke gave her the box, she said, "This box has been opened, hasn't it!" "Oh no, nothing of the sort!" protested Tōsuke. But the woman, looking extremely displeased, said, "You've done a terrible thing!" Then, with an air of profound regret, she took the box and Tōsuke went home.

After that Tōsuke, complaining that he did not feel well, took to his bed. "She said not to look, but you had to open it!" he said to his wife, and shortly after, he died.

Thus we see that when a wife has profound feelings of jealousy and acts on the basis of imaginings, she brings bad luck on the husband. Because of jealousy, Tōsuke died an unexpected and miserable death. Although they say that jealousy is just part of a woman's constant nature, still all who heard of this incident blamed the wife—so the story goes.

How a Group of Nuns Went into the Mountains, Ate Some Mushrooms, and Danced (28:28)

Long ago, some woodcutters of the capital went into the mountains north of the city to gather fuel, but they took a wrong turn and found themselves completely lost. There they were, four or five in the party, sitting in the mountains and feeling downcast, when a number of people appeared from the depths of the mountain. "Who could these people be?" they wondered, when they saw that it was a group of four or five nuns dancing around wildly.

The woodcutters, seeing them, reacted with fear and alarm. "These nuns dancing around like this—they're surely not ordinary beings! Could they be *tengu*,"[47] they wondered, "or some other sort of devilish spirits?"

When the nuns caught sight of the woodcutters, they headed straight in their direction, which terrified the woodcutters even more. As the nuns drew nearer, the woodcutters spoke to them. "What kind of nuns are you, coming out of the deepest part of the mountain and dancing around in a wild manner like this?" they asked.

"Probably it's because we are dancing around like this that you find us frightening," the nuns replied. "But we live nearby. We thought we would pick some flowers to offer to the Buddha—that's why we went off in a company like this. But then we took a wrong path and found that we didn't know the way home.

---

47. *Tengu* are goblins with wings and long noses who live in the mountains, particularly the mountains north of Kyoto.

"We came on some mushrooms, and we were hungry. We wondered if it would be all right to pick and eat them, or if perhaps they were harmful. We decided, though, that it was better to eat them than just to die of hunger. So we said, 'Well, then, let's eat them!' And when we picked some and roasted them and ate them, they turned out to be very tasty. 'They'll do just fine!' we thought, but after we'd eaten them, we found that, even though we didn't want to, we just couldn't help dancing. We knew at heart that it was a very peculiar thing to do—yes, it certainly was peculiar . . ."

Hearing this, the woodcutters were even more astounded. The nuns had a lot of mushrooms left over from the ones they had eaten. Seeing these, the woodcutters thought, "Better than dying of hunger, why don't we just eat some of those?" They asked the nuns to give them some, and after they had eaten them, they found that, in spite of themselves, they were dancing around, too. So both the nuns and the woodcutters danced together, laughing the whole while.

After some time, however, like drunken people sobering up, they came to their senses, and each group somehow was able to find its way home. From this time on, these particular mushrooms came to be called *maitake*, or "dancing mushrooms."

Thinking it over, it seems like a very odd affair. Nowadays, we have things called *maitake*, but the people who eat them do not necessarily start dancing.[48] So people say they find this whole story to be decidedly strange.

How Fujiwara no Nobutada, Governor of Shinano, Took a Tumble at Misaka (28:38)

Long ago, there was a man named Fujiwara no Nobutada,[49] governor of Shinano Province. He had traveled to Shinano, fulfilled his term as governor

48. The type of mushroom now known as *maitake* (dancing mushroom; *Grifola frondosa*), widely eaten in Japan, has no such intoxicating effect. The mushrooms the nuns ate were presumably of some variety with hallucinatory power.
49. Fujiwara no Nobutada ended his term of office as governor of Shinano in 988, so the incident related here must have taken place then or shortly after.

His retainers pull Fujiwara no Nobutada from the ravine in a basket. (From an Edo-period wood-block edition of *Konjaku monogatari shū*, with the permission of Komine Kazuaki)

there, and was on his way back to the capital. When he crossed over the pass at Misaka,[50] the horses laden with the governor's belongings and the riders in his party were too numerous to count. And among these many riders was the governor on his horse. As his horse passed over the logs at the outer edge of the trail, its hind hoof slipped and it lost its footing. The governor, horse and all, tumbled head over heels, plummeting from the path.

How deep was the ravine the governor fell into no one could tell—it was unthinkable that he could have survived. Below could be seen the topmost branches of cedars and cypresses towering a hundred feet or more, but peer as one might, one could not possibly guess how far down the bottom was. No one could imagine that the governor could take such a plunge and come out alive.

The governor's numerous retainers got off their horses and, squatting along the edge of the log trail, stared down into the ravine. The situation seemed hopeless. "Nothing we can do now!" they said. "If there was some way we could get down there, we might see what's become of the governor. Another day on the road, and we'd come to a place that's not so deep—then we could work our way back and look for him. But there's no way we can get to the bottom of the ravine from here. What's to be done?" Just then, while they were one by one mulling over the possibilities, they heard the faint sound of someone calling from deep in the ravine.

"It's his Excellency the Governor!" they exclaimed. And when they gave an answering shout, they could just hear far in the distance the governor shouting something.

"There—he's saying something. Quiet! Listen to what he's saying! He's saying, 'Tie a long rope to one of the travel baskets!' So the governor's alive—something must have broken his fall!"

Tying together the reins from a number of horses, they fashioned a rope of sorts, fastened it to one of the travel baskets, and little by little lowered

---

50. Misaka is a narrow and dangerous pass on the road between Shinano and Mino provinces, or present-day Nagano and Gifu prefectures. In steep places or where it followed the edge of a cliff, the road was paved with logs to provide better footing and to widen the path.

it. When they had paid it all out, they felt the rope go slack, so they knew that it had struck bottom.

Then they heard a voice saying, "Now pull it up!" "He's telling us to pull it up," they said. But when they did so, they found that the basket was very light in weight. "The basket's terribly light! If his Excellency were riding in it, it ought to be much heavier!" "Maybe it's light because he's grabbing hold of branches and pulling himself up," someone suggested. So they went on pulling. But when they had pulled the basket up where they could get a good look, they found it piled high with nothing but *hiratake* mushrooms.[51]

The men looked at one another in bafflement. "What in the world—?" they said. Then they heard the voice from the depths calling once more. "Lower it again!" it said.

Hearing this, they replied, "Well, then, here it goes again," and down went the basket. "Now pull it up!" said the voice. They pulled as the voice had instructed, but this time the basket was unexpectedly heavy— it took several men hauling on the rope to get it up. And when they got it up and looked, there was the governor sitting in the basket. With one hand he held fast to the rope; in the other, he grasped three bunches of *hiratake* mushrooms.

Once he had been hoisted up and was seated on the log roadway, his retainers, greatly relieved at how things had turned out, said, "Now tell us—why all these mushrooms?"

"When I fell," the governor replied, "the horse fell to the bottom faster then I did. I came tumbling down after. The branches were very thick and all twined together so they broke my fall. Grabbing hold of the branches as I was going down, I came to a branch of a big tree that gave me some footing. With the help of that, I got my arms around a branch in the fork of a tree where I came to a stop. This tree had a lot of *hiratake* mushrooms growing on it. I couldn't take my eyes off them. So I picked the ones within reach and put them in the basket and had them hauled up. But there must

---

51. The *hiratake* (oyster mushroom; *Pleurotus ostreatus*) is an edible mushroom, with a shell-like appearance, that grows on trees in the wild.

be lots more—more than one can imagine. What a loss, what a terrible loss, I kept thinking!"

"Truly a great loss indeed!" said his retainers, and they burst out laughing.

"It's no laughing matter, you fellows!" said the governor. "I felt like a man who goes into a mountain heaped with treasures and comes back empty-handed. But, as the saying goes, 'A high official never stumbles without coming up with a handful of earth.'"[52]

The chief assistant to the governor, an older man, though inwardly repelled by such an attitude, exclaimed, "How right you are! If there is anything at hand to be taken, how could you fail to take it? No one in such a situation would neglect to do so. But only a truly wise person like your Excellency would keep his wits about him in the kind of perilous situation you met with. Whatever the circumstances, you carry on as though you were dealing with everyday affairs. So, without becoming the least bit flustered, you proceeded to pick mushrooms. And you govern a province in the same way, raking in whatever good things there are to be had, taking whatever you have a mind to take. And the people of the province love and look up to you as they would their own father and mother. Therefore, may you continue in this manner for a thousand autumns, for ten thousand years!" As he spoke, the others in the group did what they could to hide their snickers.

Even in a dire situation such as this, the governor took care to first send up a load of mushrooms, a distinctly odd way of doing things when you consider it. We can only imagine how he must have snatched at things when it was easier for him to do so. People who hear of this will doubtless laugh in derision, but such is the story that has been handed down.

---

52. That is, government officials such as the governor turn every occasion into an opportunity for gain.

How a Thief Climbed to the Upper Story of Rashōmon Gate and Came on a Corpse (29:18)

Long ago, a man left Settsu Province and went to the capital in hopes of stealing something. Arriving in the capital while it was still daylight, he stood in the shadows at the foot of Rashōmon Gate.[53]

Because many people were going up and down along Shujaku Avenue, the thief decided to wait by the gate until things had quieted down. But when he heard sounds of a large number of people arriving from the area of Yamashiro to the south, he thought to himself, "Better if no one sees me!" Keeping out of sight, he managed little by little to climb up to the upper story of the gate. When he peered into the interior of the gate, he could see a faint light burning.

The thief, wondering at this, looked more carefully through the window grating. Inside lay the corpse of a young woman, and by her head a torch was burning. An old, old woman with white hair sat by the dead woman's head, yanking and pulling out handfuls of her hair.

The thief could make no sense of what he saw. "Could it be the ogre?" he thought, terror coming over him.[54] "But maybe it's only a ghost. I'll try giving it a scare!" Stealthily, he opened the door to the inner room, drew his sword, and, shouting "You—you there!" rushed in.

The old woman, greatly flustered, wrung her hands in alarm. "Who are you, old woman?" the thief demanded. "What are you doing here?"

"The lady who was my mistress has gone and left me!" said the old woman. "I've no way to bury her properly, so I've brought her here. But see her hair—how nice and long it is! I'm pulling it out so I can make a wig! Have pity on me!"

---

53. Rashōmon was the main gate on the southern side of the capital, where Shujaku (Suzaku) Avenue, which ran down the middle of the city, came to an end. From Rashōmon Gate, the avenue led north to the imperial palace.
54. Popular belief of the time held that Rashōmon Gate was inhabited by an *oni* (ogre).

The thief stripped off the clothing the corpse was wearing; seized the old woman's clothes as well, along with the handful of hair she had pulled out; climbed down the gate as fast as he could; and ran away.

There were lots of skeletons of people in the upper story of the gate. When it was impossible to give someone a proper burial, people would bring the body to the upper story of the gate and leave it there.

The thief told someone about what had happened and so word of it got around. Such, then, is the story that has been handed down.

How a Man Was Traveling with His Wife to Tanba and Got Tied Up at Ōeyama (29:23)

Long ago, there was a man of the capital whose wife came from Tanba Province. This man set out with his wife to journey to Tanba. The wife rode their horse, while the husband, a bamboo quiver with some ten arrows slung over his shoulder and carrying a bow, walked along behind. When they reached the area of Ōeyama,[55] they were joined on the road by a sturdily built young man carrying a long sword.

As the two men went along, they began a conversation, "Where are you headed?" and such like, chatting in a friendly manner. Then the man with the sword said, "This sword I'm wearing was made in Michinoku Province.[56] It's a really fine specimen—here, have a look!" He took it off and showed it to the other man; it was indeed a very fine sword.

Looking at it, the man from the capital was seized with an overwhelming desire to have it. Observing this, the young man said, "If this sword would be of any use to you, why don't you take it? And in exchange, I'll take that bow you're carrying."

55. Tanba was the province directly northwest of the capital. Ōeyama here is the hilly region between the western edge of Kyoto and present-day Kameoka.
56. Michinoku Province, in northern Japan, was famous for its swords.

The man from the capital had no great attachment to the bow he was carrying, while he regarded the sword as a real prize. In view of his great longing for the sword and his thoughts of what a wonderful acquisition it would be, he readily agreed to the exchange.

After they had walked on for a time, the young man said, "If I'm just carrying a bow, people may think it peculiar. While we're going through the mountains, why don't you let me carry a few arrows as well. That will help you out too. As long as we're going together, it's all the same thing anyway, isn't it?"

When the man from the capital heard this, he thought to himself, "Quite right!" And besides, he was so delighted at being able to carry a fine sword instead of the bow that he did as the other man suggested, taking two arrows from his quiver and handing them over. The young man, carrying the bow and with two arrows in his hand, walked behind, while the man from the capital, the quiver with the remaining arrows on his back and the sword at his waist, went ahead.

Presently, since it was time for the noon meal, they stopped at a grove of trees. "Let's not eat where people passing by can see us—let's go a little farther in," the young man said. So they went deeper into the grove. But while the man from the capital was helping his wife down from the horse, the young man suddenly fitted an arrow to the bow he was carrying, took aim at the other man, and pulled the bowstring far back. "Don't move or I'll shoot!" he said.

Taken completely by surprise, the man from the capital had no idea what to expect. He just stood there staring at the other man.

"Move along deeper into the mountains—go on!" the young man commanded in a threatening tone. Fearing for his life, the man from the capital, his wife accompanying him, went half a mile or so deeper into the mountains. "Throw me the sword and your knife!" the young man ordered, and the other man threw him both of them. The young man came forward, picked them up, and, easily overpowering the other man, tied him securely to a tree with the bridle from the horse.

The young man then went to take a closer look at the wife. She was in her twenties, a woman of humble birth but extremely beautiful and appealing. Just looking at her, his desires were aroused. Forgetting everything else, he ordered her to take off her clothes. The woman, realizing that she had no alternative, accordingly took them off. The man then took off his own clothes and forced her to submit to him. The woman had no choice— she had to do what he said. But when the man tied to the tree saw what was happening, what must he have thought?

After that, the young man got up and put his clothes back on. He slung the quiver over his shoulder, fastened the sword at his waist, took the bow in hand, and, as he mounted the horse, said to her, "I'm very sorry to leave you, but that's how things must be. I'm off now. As for that man, for your sake I'll leave him there and not kill him. I'm taking the horse so I can make a quick getaway." Then he galloped off as fast as he could, and no one knows where he went.

The woman walked over to her husband and untied him. The husband looked dazed and shamefaced. "You're completely worthless!" she said. "From now on, I'll never be able to count on you for anything!" The husband had no answer for this, and so the two of them resumed their journey to Tanba.

The young man had some sense of decency—at least he didn't rob the woman of her clothes. But the man from the capital — what hopeless stupidity! Off somewhere in the mountains, to hand your bow and arrows over to a man you've never laid eyes on before—a real idiot!

As for the other man, no one knows what became of him. This, then, is the story that's been handed down.

How a Poor Man Left His Wife and She Became the Wife of the Governor of Settsu (30:5)

Long ago in the capital, there was a young man of rather humble birth who was extremely poor. He had no friends, no father or mother or kinfolk, and no place to live. So he was obliged to live with people of another household and work for them. Because the people he worked for treated him so shabbily, he tried to find a place where he would get better treatment. But wherever he went, it was just the same. Being unfit for service in a household of the aristocracy, however, he could not hope for any improvement.

He had a wife—young, attractive in form and bearing, and refined in nature—who remained by his side, poor as he was. Troubled by his many worries, he spoke to her in this fashion: "As long as we're in this world, I'd thought that we would stay together. But we seem to grow poorer with each passing day. Since things go so badly for us together, perhaps we should try going our separate ways. What do you think?"

"I cannot see things that way," his wife replied. "Our troubles are due simply to karma from a past existence. If we are to face death by starvation, I would hope that we might face it together. But if you believe that the situation is hopeless and that it is not good for us to remain together, then perhaps we should try parting."

This was in fact what the husband wanted, and so, weeping and vowing to be true to each other, they parted.

Later the wife, who was still young and attractive in form and bearing, found employment in the household of —— of ——.[57] She was a woman highly refined in nature, and her employer, feeling sorry for her, treated her with kindness. When his own wife died, he treated her with increasing familiarity, addressing her in intimate terms. She slept by his side, and there was nothing strained or hateful in their relations. As time passed, eventually he came to regard this woman as in all respects his wife, putting her in complete charge of all his household affairs.

Around this time, the gentleman was appointed governor of Settsu Province.[58] The woman became more and more refined in bearing with the passing of the years. But her husband of former times, whose idea it had been that they should try living apart, thereafter seemed only to fall deeper and deeper into poverty. In time, he found that he could no longer remain in the capital. He made his way aimlessly to the area of Settsu, where the only employment he could find was that of field hand. He did the meanest sort of work, tilling the fields or cutting timber, but even such tasks he

57. There are blanks in the text rather than names.
58. Settsu Province was the area around the present-day city of Osaka.

could not seem to get the hang of. His employer, regarding him as next to useless, sent him to the Bay of Naniwa to cut reeds.[59]

And as he made his way there to cut reeds, the governor of Settsu, along with his wife, left the capital and journeyed to Settsu. When they reached the area of Naniwa, they halted their carriage in order to enjoy the view. Accompanied by a large number of attendants and lackeys, they ate, drank wine, and amused themselves at leisure. The governor's lady, along with her women attendants, looked out from their carriage, viewing the delights and peculiarities of the scene. There were many low-class laborers cutting reeds, but among them was one who, though no more than a hired hand, seemed to have a refined air.

The governor's lady looked at him long and carefully. "This man looks strangely like my husband of former times," she thought. Could she be mistaken? she wondered, but looking even more closely, she saw that it was indeed he. How wretched he seemed, standing there cutting reeds. "As ever, a pitiful sight!" she thought. "Has karma from a past existence brought him to this?" Her tears poured down, but, pretending that nothing was amiss, she summoned a man and said, "Among those hired laborers cutting reeds, call that fellow over here!"

The man hurried off with this message. "You there, the people in that fine carriage want you!" The reed cutter, thinking this all but impossible, stood in hesitation. But the messenger, shouting in a loud and threatening voice, said, "Hurry up now!" The man stopped cutting reeds, fastened his sickle at his waist, and went over to the carriage.

When the governor's lady saw him up close, she knew that it was him. He was smeared black with dirt and dressed in a sleeveless hemp smock that reached to his knees. He wore a battered cap; his face, hands, and feet were plastered in dirt; and he was filthy all over. Leeches had fastened themselves to the backs of his knees and shins, making bloody sores. The governor's lady, seeing him in this condition, was filled with pity. She had one of her people take him food and wine to drink, and observing his

59. The swampy area on which Osaka was later built, the Bay of Naniwa at this time was a vast plain of reeds. The cut reeds were used to make various household articles.

expression as he faced her carriage and ate and drank with gusto, she was moved to even greater pity.

To one of the women in her carriage she said, "Among those hired laborers cutting reeds, this man for some reason seems more refined. I feel very sorry for him." Taking a robe from among the things in the carriage, she said to the woman, "Here—give this to that man." And as she did so, she wrote the following words on a scrap of paper and handed it over with the robe:

Ashikaraji	No bad will come of it—
to omohite koso	so we thought
wa wakareshika	and thus we parted.
nado ka Naniwa no	Why of all things
ura ni shimo sumu	do you live in this Bay of Naniwa?

Presented with the robe, the man thought it very strange. Wondering why this had happened, he saw that there was something written on the slip of paper. Looking at it, he read what was written there. "How strange!" he thought. "This must have been written by the woman who was once my wife!" Thinking that his deeds in a past life must have brought this sorrow and shame on him, he said, "Would someone please bring me an inkstone?"[60] And when the stone was brought, he wrote these words:

Kimi nakute	Without you
ashikarikeri to	nothing good came my way.
omou ni wa	Thinking of it,
itodo Naniwa no	the life I lead in the Bay of Naniwa
ura zo sumiuki	is all the more dismal![61]

---

60. A stone on which dry ink and water are mixed, the inkstone and its writing brush allowed the man to write a reply to his former wife's poem.
61. The poems contain word plays on *ashi* (reeds) and *ashi* (bad, ill-omened).

When the governor's lady read this, she felt even sorrier for him. As for the man, he did not go back to cutting reeds but instead ran away and hid.

Afterward, the governor's lady never told anyone about this affair. For all we know, it was all due to karma from a past existence. It is senseless, therefore, to resent one's lot in life.

The governor's lady, when she grew old, must have told the story to others, and so it has been handed down and has reached those of us of a later age.

A Collection of Tales from Uji (*Uji shūi monogatari*, early thirteenth century), whose author and date of composition are uncertain, is the most popular and widely read of the medieval *setsuwa* collections. The quality of the writing was considered to be unsurpassed among *setsuwa* collections, and the book was widely printed and read in the Edo period (1600–1867). An aristocrat of the Heian period (794–1185), the Senior Counselor (*Dainagon*) Minamoto no Takakuni (1004–1077), who lived at the Byōdō-in Buddhist temple at Uji, south of the capital, is thought to have written a work entitled *Tales of the Senior Counselor* (*Uji dainagon monogatari*, late eleventh century), which was very popular but was lost. The attempt to reconstruct the lost text in the early thirteenth century probably resulted in the *Uji shūi monogatari*. The *Uji* in the title refers to the Byōdō-in, and *shūi* (collection of remains) probably refers to collecting the remains of the *Uji dainagon monogatari*.

The *Uji shūi monogatari* contains 197 stories, of which 80 also appear in *Tales of Times Now Past* (*Konjaku monogatari shū*, ca. 1120), and a number are in other *setsuwa* collections. That so many of these stories appear elsewhere is an indication of how popular they were at the time. Fifty of the stories are not duplicated in other collections, however, including humorous tales with sexual content and folktales such as "How Someone Had a Wen Removed by Demons" (3) and "How a Sparrow Repaid Its Debt of Gratitude" (48).

The stories in the *Uji shūi monogatari* are not arranged according to subject matter, as they are in the *Konjaku monogatari shū*, nor does the collection seem to have any particular order or plan, except to include the most interesting stories. The anthology contains many kinds of stories: serious and humorous, Japanese and foreign (India and China), Buddhist (about one-third to one-half), and secular, with many of the most noted being secular. Unlike the Buddhist tales in the *Konjaku monogatari shū*, the Buddhist-related stories in the *Uji shūi monogatari* do not appear to have been intended for immediate religious use. Instead, the interest is in looking at individuals and human society with an ironic eye and a love of good storytelling. Whereas in the late Heian and early Kamakura (1183–1333) periods, *setsuwa* were collected as part of the attempt to preserve artifacts of a court culture that was rapidly disappearing, in *Uji shūi monogatari* the point of view is not at all fixed, instead exploring different classes and social groups from different angles.

The stories in the *Uji shūi monogatari* are not records of oral performances but are written narratives that assume the characteristics of an oral presentation. Accordingly, the *setsuwa* open with set phrases like "Now, long ago" (*Ima wa mukashi*) and end with "so it has been told" (*to ka, to zo, to nan*). "How Someone Had a Wen Removed by Demons" (3) concludes with a didactic message, but it was probably added as part of the convention of storytelling. The story "About the Priest with the Long Nose" (25) was adapted by the novelist Akutagawa Ryūnosuke (1892–1927) into his noted short story "Nose" (Hana). Akutagawa also used "How Yoshihide, a Painter of Buddhist Pictures, Took Pleasure in Seeing His House on Fire" (38), which also appears in *A Miscellany of Ten Maxims* (*Jikkinshō*, 1252 [1:6]), for his famous short story "Hell Screen" (Jigokuhen).

The *setsuwa* "How a Sparrow Repaid Its Debt of Gratitude" (48) belongs to the long tradition of *ongaeshi* (repaying-gratitude tales) involving animals. "How a Man Received a Bounty After a Period of Prayer at the Hase Temple" (96) is about the miraculous powers of Kannon (Avalokiteśvara), the bodhisattva of mercy, at Hase Temple (in Nara) and belongs to the category of stories about the miraculous powers of a deity or a temple. A similar story appears in the *Konjaku monogatari shū* (16:28), in a section on Kannon. The real interest of this tale, however, is in the rise from poverty to wealth through a series of fortuitous exchanges, which begin with something very small (a stalk of straw and a horsefly) and gradually increase in size. Finally, "How a Priest Falsely Stated That He Would Drown Himself"

(133) is included here because it criticizes the actions of a Buddhist priest at a time when Buddhist priests and Buddhist tales were held in high esteem.

How Someone Had a Wen Removed by Demons (3)

At a time now past, there was an old man who had a large wen on the right side of his face. It was as big as a mandarin orange. This made it difficult for him to associate with others, and so, in order to support himself, he went to the mountains to gather firewood. One day, the wind and rain were so overpowering that he was unable to make his way home. Much against his wishes, he was forced to spend the night in the mountains. With no other woodcutters around, one can hardly imagine how frightening it was.

He found a tree that had a hollow and crawled into it. But, being unable to get to sleep, he pushed his way farther into the hollow until, far in the distance, he heard the sound of a large number of people noisily moving about. He had supposed that he was all alone in the mountains, and yet there seemed to be signs that others were present as well. Taking courage from this, he looked more carefully and found that he could make out demon-like creatures of all different shapes and figurations—red ones dressed in green, black ones wearing red loincloths, some with only one big eye, some with no mouth, some so strange they defied description—a hundred of them, all crowded around together. They had a fire going, like a sun in the sky, and were seated in a circle around it in front of the tree with the hollow in it. The old man was utterly astonished.

The demon who seemed to be their leader was seated at the head of the company, with the other demons ranged to the left and right, their number too great to be reckoned, their features so varied that one could never finish describing them. Wine was being passed around, and they were amusing themselves exactly as human beings do. From time to time, they exchanged wine cups, and the chief demon appeared to be drunker than the others.

From the lower end of the circle a young demon stood up alone, placed a tray on top of his head, and, chanting some kind of rigmarole over and

The demons peel the wen from the cheek of the old man. (From *Konjaku monogatari emaki*, Edo period, with the permission of Kokuritsu kokkai toshokan)

over, advanced ceremoniously to where the chief demon was seated; there he continued his chanting. The chief demon, holding his wine cup in his left hand, fell over in a fit of laughter just the way humans do.

When the young demon had finished his dance, others from the lower end of the circle one by one came forward to dance, some completely hopeless at it, others quite good. The chief demon, observing all this with surprise and delight, said, "This evening's entertainment has been even finer than usual. But I wish I could see someone perform a truly unusual dance for us!"

The old man, hearing him go on in this way, perhaps possessed by some outside force or moved to do so by the gods and buddhas, thought to himself, "Well, then, why don't I get up and dance?" He pondered this for a bit, but somehow, as he listened to the encouraging hand claps of the demons, he made up his mind: "Whatever comes, I'll just get up and dance. If it means death, then there's an end to it!" This thought in mind, the old man emerged from the hollow of the tree, his hat hanging down over his nose, the hatchet he used to cut firewood fastened at this waist, and danced his way forward to the place where the chief demon was seated.

"What's this?" cried the demons, leaping to their feet in astonishment and milling about. The old man flung up his arms, hunched his body over, and danced with all his might, posturing in every possible fashion and emitting whoops of exhilaration as he pranced and paced his way around the circle. The chief demon, along with the others in the demon company, all stared in amazement.

Then the chief demon spoke up: "Many years now we've been enjoying this sport, but never have we seen anyone like you! From now on, old man, you must make certain to join our entertainment!"

"You have only to command, and I will surely do so," the old man replied. "In my haste, I have at the moment forgotten the concluding figures of my dance. But if what I have done so far pleases you, next time I will perform in a more leisurely manner."

"Aptly spoken!" said the chief demon. "That you must surely do." But the demon in the third seat away said, "This old man has given his promise, but for all we know he may very well not keep it. He should be made to give some pledge of his fidelity!" "Quite right, quite right!" said the chief demon. "What should we ask for as a pledge?"

While the others were discussing what would be appropriate, the chief demon said, "This old man has a wen on his face—we could take that! A wen is a mark of good fortune, so he would certainly be unwilling to lose it!"[1]

"If it's only an eye or a nose you want, that's one thing," said the old man. "But when it comes to this wen, I must beg you to excuse me. It's been with me for so many years that I would be totally lost without it."

"See how loathe he is to part with it!" said the chief demon. "So that's what we must have." "Just so!" said the other demons, crowding around. "Off with it!" And they proceeded to wrench and peel it away from his face, though in fact he felt no pain at all. "And be sure to join us when we have our festivities next time!" came their voices.

Birds were singing in the dawn, and all the demons had vanished. When the old man felt his face, he could find no trace of the wen that had been there for so many years—it was as smooth as though it had been wiped clean. Forgetting all about the firewood he had intended to cut, he returned to his home. When his old wife asked, "Where have you been all this time?" he explained that this, that, and the other had happened to him. "An amazing story!" she said.

There was an old man living next door who had a big wen on the left side of his face. When he saw that the first old man had somehow gotten rid of his wen, he said, "How did you get rid of your wen? What doctor removed it for you? Please tell me so I can get mine removed too."

"It was not removed by any doctor," said the first old man. He explained that such and such had happened and that the wen had been removed by demons. "Then I'll get mine removed in the same way!" said the second old man. He asked about the exact circumstances under which the removal had taken place, and the first old man gave him instructions.

Following these, the second old man entered the hollow in the tree, waited for a while, and, just as he had been told would happen, the demons

---

1. A wen is a kind of *fukurami* (swelling) and hence perhaps suggests the word *fuku* (good fortune).

appeared. They were sitting in a circle, drinking wine and amusing themselves. "Well, well!" they exclaimed. "It's the old man!" The old man, thoroughly terrified, trembled as he approached them. "The old man's come to join us!" the demons said.

"Come here and be quick with your dancing!" said the chief demon. But this old man, unlike the earlier one, had no talent for dancing, and his movements were awkward in the extreme. "This time your dancing is abominable!" said the chief demon. "It's dreadful any way you look at it! Give him back the wen we took as a pledge last time!"

And the demons in the lower part of the circle came forward, declaring, "Very well, we hereby return the wen he gave us as a pledge!" and they proceeded to stick it onto the other side of his face. Thus the old man ended up with wens on both sides of his face. As they say, no good comes from envying others.

❋

About the Priest with the Long Nose (25)

Long ago in Ikenoo lived a Buddhist priest named Zenchin Naigu.[2] He was skilled at reciting the mantras of Esoteric Buddhism and for many years had been highly esteemed for this ability. Thus the people of the time frequently requested him to offer prayers of various kinds for them. He was therefore very well off, and his Buddhist halls and living quarters were kept in excellent repair. His altars were never lacking in offerings and votive lights, and there were ample meals for his temple personnel and frequent meetings held at the temple to expound the doctrine, so the temple's living quarters were at all times bustling with clergy in residence. Not a day passed when the water in the temple bathhouse was not heated and there were not crowds of bathers there. Moreover, many small houses had been built in the vicinity of the temple, and the whole village prospered because of it.

2. Ikenoo is in Uji. The title Naigu (Palace Chaplain) indicates that he was qualified to take part in religious activities in the imperial palace, a mark of high honor.

The young acolyte holds up the nose of Zenchin with a flat board while the priest eats. (From an Edo-period wood-block edition of *Uji shūi monogatari*, with the permission of Komine Kazuaki)

As it happened, Priest Zenchin's nose was very long. It measured some five or six inches in length, and seemed to droop down below his chin. It was reddish-purple in color and had bumps on it like the rind of a large mandarin orange. And it was intolerably itchy. He would take a container for heating liquids, fill it with water, and bring the water to a boil. Then he would take a wooden tray with a small hole in it just big enough to fit his nose and, using the tray to protect his face from the steam, insert his nose through the hole and down into the hot water in the container. After he had steeped his nose in the hot water for a considerable time, he would pull it out and it would be a deep purple in color.

He would then lie down on his side, put a board under his nose, and have someone trample on it. Each of the bumps on his nose would then emit something that looked like steam. If the person trampled hard, white worms would come out of all the holes. Using tweezers to pull them, you could pull a white worm one or two inches in length out of each hole. After that the holes stayed open. If Zenchin put his nose back in the hot water and heated the water to boiling point, the nose would shrink to the size of an ordinary person's nose. But after two or three days, it would once again get as big as it had been before.

As a result, most days Zenchin's nose was large in size. At mealtime, he would have a young disciple monk sit beside him holding a flat board an inch in width and about a foot long. Thrusting the board under the nose, the monk would lift it up out of the way so that Zenchin could finish his meal. If anyone else tried to perform the task, his lack of skill in handling the board made Zenchin so angry that he could not eat his food. Therefore, he always had this disciple monk hold the board when it came time to eat.

It so happened, however, that this disciple monk was one time taken ill and there was no one to hold up the board so Zenchin could eat his morning bowl of rice gruel. "What am I to do now!" Zenchin fretted. The boy who delivered word of the illness later said, "I could perfectly well hold up the board. I'm sure I could do just as well as the distinguished gentleman who usually does it!" The disciple monk, hearing of this remark, informed Zenchin of what the boy had said. The boy was of a certain standing among the acolytes, and moreover was not unattractive in appearance, and he was accordingly summoned to Zenchin's quarters. He picked up the board that held up the nose, positioned himself properly in his seat, and held the board just right, not too high and not too low. As Zenchin began to eat the gruel in a slurping fashion, he said, "This boy is really good! He's even better than the monk who usually waits on me!"

But while Zenchin was slurping away, the boy felt a tickling in his nostril. Turning to one side, he gave a loud sneeze. As he did so, his hand shook, and Zenchin's nose slipped off the board and fell with a plop into the bowl of gruel. Both Zenchin's face and that of the boy were splattered all over with blobs of rice gruel.

Zenchin was enraged. As he wiped the gruel from his scalp and face with a piece of paper, he said, "You are an utterly evil-hearted wretch! No better than the most ignorant beggar brat! If you were to attend the nose of someone, unlike myself, who was vastly your superior, would you do this kind of thing? You're nothing but a brainless idiot—get out, get out!"

Driven from the room, the boy said, "If there are any others who want to come and hold up his honorable nose, they're welcome to the job. I've had enough of this drivel-mouthed bonze!" At these words, all the other disciples, fleeing to a place where they couldn't be heard, broke down in laughter.[3]

How Yoshihide, a Painter of Buddhist Pictures, Took Pleasure in Seeing His House on Fire (38)

Long ago, there was a painter of Buddhist pictures named Yoshihide. Fire broke out in the house next to his, and as it was being spread by the wind, he fled from his own house and took refuge in the broad avenue in front. He had valuable Buddhist paintings in his house that he had been asked to work on, and his wife and children, lacking proper clothes to appear in public, were still in the house. But he never bothered about them, thinking it quite sufficient to dash out alone and stand on the far side of the avenue.

---

3. Part of the humor derives from the sudden and deplorable change in Zenchin's attitude. The prohibition against anger was one of the ten most important precepts of Buddhism.

And as he stood watching, he saw that the fire had already spread to his own house. Smoke and flames were shooting out of the house, yet he merely stood there staring.

"How terrible!" people said, gathering around in sympathy, but he was not frantic. "What happened?" they asked, but he simply stood there watching his house burn down. He nodded his head, and now and then laughed. "Ah, what a wonderful lesson I've learned!" he said. "All these years I've been painting them the wrong way."

At this, the people who had gathered around said, "What are you saying? A terrible thing like this—how can you just stand there? Has some spirit taken possession of you?"

"Why would you think me possessed?" he said. "For years now, I've painted the flames that surround the deity Fudō in the wrong way.[4] But now I see what real fire is like. I've learned the key to it. That's the wonderful lesson! When one sets out to make a living by my kind of work, if one can just paint the Buddhist deities in a convincing way, then one can have hundreds and thousands of houses. But you guys—you have no talent at all! That's why you're so attached to objects!" he said, and stood there laughing scornfully.

It must have been after this that Yoshihide painted *The Flame-Adorned Fudō*, which even today has so many admirers.

How a Sparrow Repaid Its Debt of Gratitude (48)

Long ago, on a spring day when the sun was shining brightly, an old woman of about sixty sat and picked lice out of her clothing. A sparrow was hopping around in her garden when a child picked up a stone and threw it at the bird. The stone struck the bird and broke its back. It fluttered its wings in helpless confusion, while crows wheeled ominously above. "Ah, poor

---

4. Fudō (Acalanātha), "the Immovable," is one of the most important guardian deities of the Buddhist religion. He is customarily depicted in a threatening posture, holding a sword and backed by raging flames.

thing!" said the woman. "The crows will get it!" and she rushed to the rescue. She managed to calm it down and gave it something to eat, putting it in a little pail and leaving it like that overnight. The next day, she fed it some rice and copper shavings as medicine.[5] Her children and grandchildren laughed at her scornfully, saying, "Just look at Grandmamma—she's taken to raising sparrows in her old age!"

After a few months had passed in this way, the sparrow bit by bit got so it could hop around. And in its heart, it felt unending gratitude for the care that it had received. As for the old woman, whenever she went somewhere, she would always leave word with others, saying, "Look out for the sparrow—see that it has something to eat." Her children and grandchildren laughed with scorn. "Why worry so much about a sparrow?" they said. She replied, "You're right, but it's such a pitiful little thing!"

As a result of this care, the sparrow in time was able to fly once more. "Now it probably won't be at the mercy of the crows," said the old woman, and she took it outdoors and held it up on her hand. "You can fly all right now—just try!" she said. And as she held it up, the bird fluttered its wings and flew away. "All these months," said the old woman, "when night came I'd always put it in the house, and next morning I'd give it its food. And now look—it's flown away! Will it come again? I'll have to wait and see." Left with so little to do, she kept thinking of it, while the others laughed at her.

Some twenty days later, a sparrow was making a great deal of noise in the vicinity where the old woman lived. "That's a very noisy sparrow," she thought. "I wonder if my sparrow has come?" And when she went out to see, it was indeed her sparrow. "Just look!" she said. "It hasn't forgotten me—it's come after all!"

The sparrow looked closely at the old woman's face, and then it dropped something from its beak that resembled a drop of dew. Then it flew away. "What could it be—this thing the sparrow's left?" she said. And when she looked, she found that it had dropped a single gourd seed. "If the bird has brought it, there must be a reason," she thought, and she carefully picked

5. Copper shavings were believed to be efficacious in healing broken bones.

up the seed. "Of all things!" said her children, laughing. "She treats the seed the sparrow brought as though it were some kind of treasure!" "Never mind," said the old woman. "I'll just try planting it."

So she planted it, and by the time autumn came, it had grown into a big flourishing plant, not at all like an ordinary gourd vine, and it bore lots of large fruit. The old woman was delighted and shared the gourds with her neighbors in the village. But as many as she picked from the vine, there were always plenty left. Even her children and grandchildren, who had laughed at her before, ate them from morning to night. She handed them out to the whole village, and in the end she set aside seven or eight of the largest and finest ones to use as containers, hanging them up in her house.

After a few months, she said, "They must be dry by now," and, examining them, she found that they were. But when she took one of them down and prepared to cut off the top, the gourd seemed rather heavy. Wondering at this, she cut it open and saw that it was full of something. "What could it be?" she thought, and, pouring out the contents, she discovered that the gourd was full of polished rice. Surprised at this unexpected discovery, she tried to empty the entire contents into another container, yet the gourd remained as full as it had been before. "There's something strange here—it must be the sparrow's doing!" she exclaimed, both puzzled and delighted. She put the rice from the first gourd in containers and stored it, and when she examined the other gourds, she found that they, too, were full of rice.

She kept pouring the rice into containers and using it up, but it always remained as plentiful as before. As a result, in time she became very wealthy, and her neighbors in the village eyed her with wonder and envy.

There was another old woman living next door to the first one, and her children said, "Both are old women, but the one next door gets rich, while ours does nothing at all for us!" The second old woman went to the woman next door. "Well, now, how are things with you? I've heard something about this sparrow affair, but I don't know the details. Tell me the whole story."

"The sparrow brought a gourd seed and I tried planting it," said the first old woman, but she did not elaborate. "Come now, tell me exactly what happened!" demanded the second old woman. The first old woman thought it wouldn't be right to be secretive and hide anything, and so she said, "The sparrow happened to get its back broken, and I nursed it back to health. It was grateful for that and brought me a gourd seed. I planted the seed and this is what happened."

"Just give me one of those seeds," said the second old woman. "I'll give you as much of the rice from the gourds as you like," the first old woman replied. "But I can't give you any seeds. It wouldn't be right to scatter them around."

Unable to get any seeds, the second old woman thought, "Then I'll find a sparrow with a broken back and nurse it back to health!" But although she looked everywhere, she couldn't find a sparrow that had a broken back.

Each morning on the lookout, she one day saw some sparrows hopping around her back garden and eating rice that had been spilled there. She picked up several stones and, thinking that she might just manage a hit, threw them one after another into the crowd of sparrows. One of the sparrows was in fact struck and could not fly away. The old woman, delighted, came closer and hit it again to make certain its back was broken. After that, she fed it, gave it some medicine, and looked after it.

"If so much good fortune comes from just one bird," she thought, "think how much I'll get if I look out for a number of them! I'll be even better off than the woman next door, and my children will sing my praises!" So she scattered rice around her garden and waited, and when a number of sparrows appeared, she threw one stone after another and succeeded in hitting three of them. "That's enough for now," she thought, and put the three sparrows with broken backs into a pail and fed them copper shavings. After a few months, all of them had recovered from their injuries. Delighted, the old woman took them outside and let them loose, and they fluttered their wings and flew away. "There," thought the old woman, "I've done a marvelous thing!" But the sparrows, having had their backs broken and been penned up for so many months, were seething with hatred.

When ten days had passed, the three sparrows came again. The old woman, overjoyed, looked first to see if they had anything in their beaks. Each, in fact, had a single gourd seed, which it dropped and then flew away. "Here we go!" thought the old woman delightedly, and she planted the three seeds. They sprouted, grew much better than ordinary plants, and soon were very large. But they did not produce many gourds—only seven or eight. The old woman, observing them with a smile, said to her children, "I didn't say I could do anything wonderful, but at least I've outdone the woman next door!" "We hope so," thought her children.

Because the gourds were so few in number, she wanted to get as much rice as possible from them. So she did not give any of the gourds to others or eat any of them herself. Her children said, "The old woman next door gave gourds to the neighbors and fed them to her own family. And you have three gourd vines. You ought to be able to feed your own family and others as well." "All right, I'll feed the neighbors, and my children and I will eat our fill!" thought the old woman. Accordingly, she cooked a number of gourds. But when people tried to eat them, they found them horribly bitter, with a taste like *kihada* that made them nauseated.[6] Everyone who ate them—the old woman's children, the old woman herself—got sick and threw up. The neighbors, too, sickened and in misery, flocked around in anger. "What's this you've given us to eat?" they said. "It's horrible! Even those who only get close enough to sniff the odor when it's cooking throw up and act as though they're dying!" But by this time, the old woman, along with her children, were sprawled on the ground, so nauseated that they hardly knew what was happening. With nowhere to deliver their complaints, the neighbors returned home.

By the time two or three days had passed, everyone had recovered from the ill effects of the gourds. The old woman thought to herself, "It's because we supposed that the ingredients in the gourds had already turned to rice and ate it too quickly that we met with this peculiar outcome!" Accordingly, she picked the rest of the gourds and set them aside.

After a few months had passed, she said, "They must be ready by now," and she brought some pails to the room, intending to empty the contents of the gourds into them. Then, her toothless old mouth opened in a grin of delight so broad that it reached to her ears, laughing to herself, she set about to empty the gourds into the pails. But instead of rice, out of the gourds came horseflies, hornets, centipedes, lizards, and vipers. They not only attacked her eyes and nose, but stung her all over her body. The old

---

6. *Kihada* is the bark of the Chinese cork tree, a bitter ingredient used in Chinese medicine.

woman, however, was not aware of the pain. Her only worry was that some of the rice would get spilled. "Wait a moment, you sparrows!" she said. "Let me have it a little bit at a time!"

Out of the seven or eight gourds came so many poisonous creatures that they stung the old woman's children all over, and in fact stung the old woman to death. The sparrows, deeply resentful at having had their backs broken, had summoned these countless noxious creatures and filled the gourds with them.

The sparrow rescued by the woman next door, by contrast, had already had its back broken and was about to be killed by crows. And because the old woman nursed it back to health, it felt great gratitude. So we know that it does not do to be envious of the good fortune of others.

How a Man Received a Bounty After a Period of Prayer at the Hase Temple (96)

Long ago, there was a young samurai of low status who was all alone in the world, with no father or mother, no lord to serve under, no wife or children. Having no one at all to turn to, he made a pilgrimage to Hase Temple and, throwing himself down before the statue, said, "Kannon, please help me! If it is my fate to suffer in this world like this, then let me die of starvation here before you. And if by chance there is some way I can escape that end, then I will not leave here until it has been revealed to me in a dream."[7]

Seeing him prostrate before the statue, the priests of the temple said, "Who are you, behaving in a fashion like this? You do not seem to be eating anything, and if you go on lying here, your death will ritually pollute the temple, a very serious matter. Who is your teacher in the faith? Who is responsible for feeding you?" But to their queries, he only replied, "How

---

7. Hase is a famous Buddhist temple in the mountains south of Nara. From early times, it has been the object of pilgrimages. It houses a statue of Kannon (the bodhisattva Avalokiteśvara), or Perceiver of the World's Sounds, who is believed to heed the cries of sufferers and grant them aid.

could a destitute person like myself have a teacher? I have no one to feed me, and if no one will have pity and give me something to eat, I must rely on what the Buddha gives me and make the Buddha my teacher."

The priests of the temple gathered around. "This is a grave matter," they said, "and likely to cause the temple much trouble. This man is trying to lay the blame for his misfortunes on Kannon. We had better see to his feeding ourselves!" So they took turns bringing him something to eat, and as a result he was able to remain in his place before the statue for a period of twenty-one days.

On the night when the twenty-one-day period was coming to an end, the man dreamed that a figure emerged from the curtains hanging before the statue and said, "Young man, you fail to realize that your plight is due to misdeeds in a previous existence and are trying to shift the blame to Kannon, a very unreasonable procedure. However, because your pleas are pitiful in nature, a certain amount of leeway has been granted you. Now listen—you must leave here immediately. And when you leave, whatever you happen to touch, no matter what it may be, you must not throw it away but keep it in your hand and hurry on your way!" The figure then made as though to drive him away. The man accordingly got up from his prostrate position, went to the priests who had been feeding him, begged some food from them, and left the temple. As he was going out the main gate, he stumbled and fell to the ground.

When he got to his feet again, he found that he was holding in his hand a single stamen from a rice plant, though he could not remember having picked it up. "Is this what the Buddha gives me?" he wondered, regarding it with disappointment and disdain. "Still," he thought, "it may be part of some plan the Buddha has for me," and he twirled it in his fingers as he walked along. Just then, a horsefly began to buzz noisily around his face. Annoyed, he broke off a little branch of a tree and tried to use it to drive away the fly. But the fly kept up its bothersome buzzing until he seized it, wrapped the rice straw around its middle, and fastened the straw to the end of the branch. The fly, unable to escape, flew in circles around the branch.

Just then a woman's oxcart appeared, on its way on a pilgrimage to Hase Temple, with a little boy peering out from the rear curtains, a charming sight. "What is that thing that man is carrying?" the boy said to the samurai who, mounted on a horse, was accompanying the oxcart. "I want one like that!" The samurai, addressing the poor man, said, "Our young master wants that thing you are carrying in your hand." "This is a gift from the Buddha," replied the poor man. "However, if you really want it, I will heed your request," and he handed it over. "You are very accommodating— surrendering in this way what our young master has asked for," said the samurai. Then he took three large mandarin oranges, wrapped them in expensive paper from Michinoku Province, and handed them to the poor man. "Eat these when you feel thirsty," he said.

"For one wisp of rice straw I got three mandarin oranges!" thought the man, and, fastening the oranges to a stick, he slung them over his shoulder and resumed his walk. As he did so, he saw a woman, apparently of high birth, who was walking on foot, accompanied by a number of samurai and other attendants.[8] She seemed to be having great trouble walking and to be on the verge of collapse. "I'm so thirsty—give me water!" she said, as though about to faint away. Her attendants, much flustered, looked around frantically for water but could find none. "What shall I do? Isn't there water with the horses we brought from the inn?" she asked. "But the horses are far behind—not even in sight," her people replied. The whole company seemed to be completely at a loss as to what to do.

Seeing that they were distressed because of the woman's thirst, the poor man approached in a tentative manner. "This man must know where there's water!" they said. "Is there anywhere close by with drinking water?" "There's no drinking water within miles of here. Why do you ask?" said the poor man. "This woman is worn out from walking. She's thirsty and needs water. If we can't find any water it will be a serious matter—that's why we ask," they replied.

"That's a pity," said the poor man. "The only water is a long way away, and it would take time to fetch it. But how would these do?" and he offered them the three mandarin oranges wrapped in paper.

Delighted at this, the attendants hurried to feed the oranges to the woman. When they had done so, after a time she opened her eyes. "What

8. Although a woman of means, she evidently was proceeding on foot as a sign of respect for Hase Temple, to which she was journeying.

happened?" she said. "You were thirsty and kept asking for water," her attendants said, "and then you lost consciousness. We tried to find some water, but there was no drinking water to be had. Then a certain man, seeing what the trouble was, quite unexpectedly presented us with three mandarin oranges, which we gave you to eat."

"So I was very thirsty, and then I lost consciousness. I recall begging for water, but I cannot remember anything after that. If I had not gotten the oranges, I probably would have died here in the wilds. How grateful I am to that man! Is he still around?" she asked. "He's right here," they replied. "Tell him not to go away," she said. "Whatever blessings I might have hoped for from my pilgrimage, if I had died here, it would all have been in vain. We must think of some way to repay the man. What can we do when we are on a journey like this? Does he seem to have anything to eat? If not, give him some food."

"You there," said the attendants. "Wait a bit. The horses from the inn will soon be here, and then we will give you something to eat." "Whatever you say," the man replied, and after a while the horses from the inn and those carrying the baggage arrived.

"Why were the horses so far behind?" the attendants grumbled. "The horses from the inn should always go ahead. We may suddenly need something they are carrying, and what can we do if they're so far behind?" In time, they managed to put up the hangings and spread out the sitting mats. "The water is still some way off, but you must be tired, so we will serve you something to eat here," said the attendants as they went to fetch water and prepared the food to be served. The poor man, as he ate his fill of the splendid meal, thought to himself, "What will they do about the oranges? I came into possession of them as part of Kannon's plan, so this can hardly be the end of the affair." As he was thinking this, the woman brought out three bolts of fine white cloth and said, "Give these to the man. I cannot thank him enough for the gift of the oranges, but as we are now on a journey, I have no way to express my true gratitude. He must look on these as no more than a mere token of my thanks. My home in the capital is at such-and-such a place. He should by all means call on me there, and I will reward him properly for the oranges." Presented with three bolts of cloth, the man accepted them with delight. "For one wisp of rice straw I now acquire three bolts of cloth!" he thought as he put them under his arm and started on his way. The day was coming to a close as he did so.

He found lodging that night in a house by the road, and the next morning was up with the birds and on his way. After the sun came up, at the Hour of the Dragon or around eight,[9] a man came along riding on a horse of superlative quality. Taking care to spare the horse, he was not galloping but proceeding at a leisurely gait. The poor man, looking at the horse, thought, "What a splendid animal! It must be worth thousands of strings of coins!" Just then, the horse suddenly fell over dead. The rider, dumbfounded at what had happened, managed to dismount and get to his feet. His attendants, likewise taken completely by surprise, came forward to remove the saddle. "What shall we do?" they exclaimed, but as the horse was already dead, there was nothing they could do but stand around helpless, clapping their hands in despair. The rider of the dead horse, since he had no other choice, mounted another beast of greatly inferior quality.

As he was about to leave, he said to one of his lackeys, "There's no point in my remaining, so I'm on my way. Just see that the horse is somehow moved out of sight," and he rode off. Observing this, the poor man thought, "I wonder if this horse didn't die so it could come into my hands? One wisp of straw turned into three oranges. Three oranges turned into three bolts of cloth. Surely now the cloth will bring me a horse!" Approaching closer, he said to the lackey, "What sort of horse is this?" "It came from the province of Michinoku," the lackey replied. "Any number of people were eager to have it, offering to buy it at whatever price. But my master wouldn't think of letting it go. Now that it's dead, though, it wouldn't fetch a fraction of the sums they offered! I'd like to at least flay it for the hide, but what would I do with it while I'm on the road? So I just stand here staring at the corpse."

"Exactly what I was thinking," said the poor man. "I can see that it's a splendid horse, but now, alas, it's dead. That's the fate that awaits all living creatures. And since you are on a journey, how in the world would you find any way to dry and cure the hide? I live nearby, so perhaps you would give me permission to flay it and make use of the hide." And as he said this, he held out a bolt of cloth as payment. The lackey, surprised to find that he

9. The Hour of the Dragon is 7:00 to 9:00 A.M.

could actually profit from the transaction, accepted the cloth, afraid only that the man would change his mind, and, without once looking back, hurried on his way.

After making certain that the lackey was out of sight, the poor man washed his hands, faced in the direction of Hase Temple, and voiced this prayer: "Please bring this horse back to life!" He had no sooner done so than the horse opened its eyes, lifted its head, and struggled to get up. With a boost from the man, it rose to its feet. The man, pleased beyond measure, thought, "Other people may be coming along, or that fellow might return!" Conscious of such dangers, he moved to a spot where he and the horse would be out of sight and rested for a while. When the horse had fully recovered, he led it to a place where there were tradesmen, exchanged a bolt of cloth for a bit and a cheap saddle, mounted the horse, and rode off.

Heading for the capital, the man had ridden as far as Uji by the time the sun went down. That night, he found lodging in a nearby house and exchanged a bolt of cloth for fodder for the horse and something to eat for himself. The next morning, he set off very early for the capital. Around the vicinity of Kujō,[10] he came upon a house whose owner was preparing to go somewhere. "I could go on to the capital," thought the poor man, "but there might be people there who know the horse and think that I stole it, which would not be good. I wonder if I couldn't sell it?" Looking around for someone who might want a horse, he dismounted and casually approached the owner of the house. "Would you like to buy a horse?" he asked. A horse was in fact just what the man needed. "How much is it?" he asked excitedly. "At the moment, I don't have any silk or other goods to pay for it, but I could give you some of the rice fields and rice around Toba in exchange for it."[11] The poor man had bigger things than silk in mind, but he said, "Actually silk or money is what I need. Since I'm on a trip, I don't know what I would do with rice fields. However, if you really need the horse, I suppose I could go along with your offer."

The owner of the house mounted the horse and tried riding it around. "As fine as I could have hoped for!" he exclaimed. Then he arranged to give

10. Kujō (Ninth Avenue) was the southern limit of the capital.
11. Toba is the agricultural region just south of the capital.

the poor man three *chō*[12] of rice fields in nearby Toba and added some rice plants and polished rice to the bargain. In the end, he turned his house over to the man as well. "If I live long enough to come back to the capital, you can return the house to me then," he said. "And if I don't come back, you can go on living here. If I should die meanwhile, the house will be yours. I don't have any children, so there would be no one else to claim it." Thus he left the poor man in charge of the house and shortly after departed from the capital.

The poor man moved into the house and stored the rice and rice plants, and since there was only himself to feed, he had plenty to eat. In the meantime, some of the local people came to work for him, so he was able to live very comfortably.

When the Second Month planting season came around, he lent out half of the fields he had received to others to cultivate, and kept half for his own use. The fields farmed by others did well enough, producing what was an average crop for the time. His own fields, however, were quite amazingly productive, and he harvested any number of rice plants and stored them. From this time on, good fortune, as though blown by the wind, seemed to gather around him, and he became a man of great wealth. No word ever came from the former owner, and the man thus gained full possession of the house. In time, he acquired children and grandchildren and is said to have prospered in a quite remarkable fashion.

How a Priest Falsely Stated That He Would Drown Himself (133)

This, too, happened long ago. A saintly member of the Buddhist clergy announced that he would drown himself in the Katsura River.[13] Before

---

12. A *chō*, here a measure of land area (not of length), is about two and a half acres. Three *chō* would not have been a very large plot, although presumably its value was enhanced by its proximity to the capital.

13. The Katsura is a shallow river that flows south on the western side of Kyoto. At the time of the story, it was widely believed that persons who called on the aid of Amida Buddha would at death be reborn in Amida's Western Paradise, where enlightenment is relatively easy to achieve. Some people, unwilling to await a natural death, committed suicide as a mark of their faith in Amida's power.

he did so, however, he held a hundred-days repentance service at Gidarin Temple.[14] People flocked from near and far to attend, and the endless procession of carriages carrying women eager to express their devotion made the roads all but impassable.

Look at him and you see a priest something over thirty, slender in build. He does not look others directly in the eye but keeps his eyes half closed, and from time to time speaks the words "Amida Buddha!" In between such utterances, you just see his lips moving, presumably because he is reciting the *nembutsu.*[15] At other times, he heaves a deep sigh and gazes about at the faces of those gathered around him. At such moments, those in his presence crowd closer, pushing and jostling for position, endeavoring to catch his eye.[16]

At dawn of the day scheduled for the suicide, the priest entered the hall of the temple, where a number of other priests had gathered, and they formed a long procession emerging from the temple. At the tail end of the procession, the priest rode in a baggage cart, dressed in paper robes and a surplice. His lips appeared to be uttering words of some kind. He did not look directly at those about him, but now and then heaved a profound sigh.

The crowds that had gathered along the way to watch threw handfuls of rice that pelted him like showers of hail.[17] But from time to time he would say, "Oh no—these only get in my eyes and nose and trouble me greatly! If you wish to make a contribution, please wrap your offerings in a paper envelope and deliver them to the temple where I have been residing." At these words, all the dullards in the crowd pressed their palms together in reverent awe. But those who were a bit brighter whispered among themselves. "That's strange!" they said. "Why does the holy man say that? He's on his way now to drown himself, yet he says to send the rice offerings to the Gidarin because they get in his eyes and nose and bother him!"

14. Gidarin Temple, founded in 1000 C.E., was in the southeastern section of the capital. The hundred-day service involved the recitation of the Lotus Sutra and the performance of rites of repentance.
15. The recitation of the words *Namu Amida Butsu,* or "Hail to Amida Buddha," is the main devotional practice of the followers of Amida.
16. Catching his eye would form a bond with him and confer a blessing.
17. Their offerings were in recognition of the religious act that he was about to perform.

The procession advanced along Shichijō[18] until the participants reached the west end of the avenue. Here were gathered even greater crowds than in the capital, more people than there were stones in the riverbed, all come to offer obeisance and watch "the holy man enter the water." The carts and carriages that had carried the participants were pushed onto the bank of the river, whereupon the holy man asked, "What time is it now?" The priests attending him replied, "The Hour of the Monkey is drawing to a close."[19] "It's too early for rebirth in the Western Paradise," said the holy man. "Let's wait until a little later." Some of those who had come a long way to observe the proceedings, tired of waiting, gave up and went home, and the crowd in the riverbed thinned out somewhat. But others, determined to see how things would turn out, remained standing. Among the priests in the company, some muttered, "Is there a fixed time for rebirth in the Western Paradise? We never heard of that!"

After some time had passed, [the party having set out in a boat,] the holy man, stripped down to a loincloth, faced west and dove plop into the water. But his foot became entangled in a line on the gunwale of the boat and he hung there, thrashing around without going under the surface. One of his disciples freed his foot, whereupon he toppled head over heels into the river, gasping and floundering about. A man who, hoping to get a better view, had climbed down into the riverbed and was standing in a shallow spot nearby took hold of the holy man's hand and pulled him to his feet. The priest, using both hands, wiped the water from his face, spat out a mouthful of river water. and, turning to the man who had pulled him out of the water and rubbing his palms together in appreciation, said, "I am immensely grateful to you! I will repay your kindness when I reach the Western Paradise!" Then he scrambled as fast as he could up the riverbank.

The people who had gathered to watch, along with the young boys in the crowd, began to pick up stones from the riverbed and shower the holy man with them. The "Master of the Dharma," naked, raced off down the

18. Shichijō (Seventh Avenue) was one of the main east–west streets in the capital. The Katsura River was situated at the western end of the avenue.
19. The Hour of the Monkey is 3:00 to 5:00 P.M.

riverbed, the onlookers one after another hurling stones after him until they had smashed him in the head.

This must be the Master of the Dharma whom people are referring to when they send a gift of a melon from Yamato and write in the message that accompanies it, "This goes in the water, like His Eminence of recent times."[20]

20. Melons, a specialty of Yamato Province, customarily are chilled in water before being eaten.

A Companion in Solitude (*Kankyo no tomo*, ca. 1222) is a two-volume collection of Buddhist *setsuwa* written by Priest Keisei (1189–1268). The twenty-one stories in volume 1 are about noted recluses and priests such as Kūya (903–972). Volume 2, by contrast, contains eleven stories about women and their search for religious enlightenment. The collection is unusual in that nearly an entire volume is devoted to female protagonists.

As Rajyashree Pandey points out, one of the central religious tropes around which these stories are organized is the notion of woman as the embodiment of the seven grave vices, a Buddhist-inflected view that had a profound impact on medieval discourse. The seven vices are having no hesitation in arousing sexual desire in men, being susceptible to jealousy, being deceitful, being given to self-adornment to seduce men, being trapped in the sin of attachment, allowing uncontrolled desire to result in shameless action, and being bodily unclean (due to menstruation and childbirth).[1] The perceived impure and sinful nature of women was, in turn, thought to prevent them from achieving immediate buddhahood. The story "How a Woman Out of Deep Resentment Changed into a Demon in Her Present Existence" (2:3) looks at what happens to a woman's body as a result of her succumbing to one of these vices. Confrontation with a decaying body was often used as a means to awaken the observer to the true nature of the human body, particularly that of women. In the tale "How a Court Lady of Royal Birth Demonstrated the Foulness of Her Bodily Form" (2:9), which

---

1. Rajyashree Pandey, "Women, Sexuality, and Enlightenment: *Kankyo no Tomo*," *Monumenta Nipponica* 50, no. 3 (1995): 325–356.

expands on the notion of impurity in woman, a refined woman decides to cure a transgressive priest of his deluded attachment to her by presenting herself to him as a repugnant and putrid figure.

How a Woman Out of Deep Resentment Changed into a Demon in Her Present Existence (2:3)

This is reported to have happened in Mino Province some time ago. It concerns a man of no little social standing who had been in the habit of making frequent visits to a certain man's daughter at her parents' home in that province.[2] But he had to go a considerable distance and could not visit her as often as he would have liked. She, perhaps because she was not familiar with the manner in which such liaisons were conducted, became thoroughly disheartened with the way their affair was progressing. And in their meetings, infrequent as they were, she seemed to see signs of waning affection. The man, too, became fearful of where the affair was heading.

As the grasses wither when winter comes, so their relationship withered away, and the woman ceased to eat anything at all. And as, with the arrival of spring, people become engrossed in their various tasks, so those around the woman, busy as they were, failed even to notice that she had stopped eating.

She spent all her time hidden behind screens, wrapped in layers of bedding, and others in the house, heartless, took no further notice of her. Then one day, someone left a bucket of sweet syrup near where she was hiding. Seizing the bucket, she twisted her hair into the shape of five topknots and plastered them with syrup, so when they dried, they stood up like horns. No one in the household was even aware of what she was doing. Then she put on a pair of scarlet trousers, crept out of the house, and disappeared.[3]

2. Following earlier Japanese custom, the man courts the woman by paying clandestine visits to her in her home, arriving at night and stealing away the following morning.

3. She has taken on the form and the attire of an avenging demon.

No one knew what had become of her. "She's just disappeared," they said. "All because of that worthless man, she probably gave up in despair and threw herself into some river or deep pond!" Although they searched for her body, they of course were never able to find it. And so time went by, the months and years piled up, until the woman's parents had passed away.

It must have been some thirty years later when, in the same province, word got around that there was a demon living in a half-ruined Buddhist hall that stood far out in the fields. Everyone said that it lived by seizing and feeding on the young of the horses and cows raised in the area. "It hides up in the ceiling of the hall," reported persons who had observed the building from a distance.

A number of the villagers got together to discuss the matter. "If that's the case, why don't we just set fire to the hall? We can pitch in later and rebuild it. Only if we burned it out of ill will toward the Buddha would there be any blame in it!" They fixed on a day for the action, and then armed themselves with bows and quivers, filled in whatever gaps there were in their protective clothing, and gathered around.

They had set fire to the hall and it was half burned when a creature, indescribably weird, with five horns on its head and dressed in scarlet trousers, came rushing down from the ceiling of the hall. "That must be it!" they exclaimed, aiming their bows at it.

"Give me a moment to speak!" said the creature. "Don't kill me before I've had a chance to explain!"

"What sort of being are you?" they asked.

"I am the daughter of So-and-so of such-and-such a place," the creature said. "Giving way to feelings that I now regret, I carried out various actions, leaving my home to do so. And in the end, I killed that man I was involved with. After that, I found that I could never return to my original form. I couldn't bear to let ordinary people see me, I had no place to go, and so I hid myself in this hall of worship. But then, how hard it was for me to stay alive! My hunger at times was more than I could bear; everything about my life was a trial—I can't tell you what hardships I endured! Night and day, my body seemed consumed in flames—regrets, evils that never came to an end.

"So I beg you, people, come together, whatever you do, and with all your hearts spend one whole day writing out passages from the Lotus

Sutra for my sake, a final memorial in my name. And those among you, those who have wives and children—you must see that my story is spread abroad as widely as possible. Warn people that they must never under any circumstances do as I have done!"

And when she had spoken these words, tears streaming down her face, she leaped into the flames and burned to death.

It was a frightening affair, but at the same time a sad one. Deeply vexed in spirit, she had allowed herself to be led astray by a moment's misapprehension, and thus condemned herself to long years of suffering. How regrettable, and how tragic! It is hardly likely that she fared well in her next existence. Perhaps prayers were said on her behalf, though I do not recall the person who told me her story making any mention of them.

How a Court Lady of Royal Birth Demonstrated the Foulness of Her Bodily Form (2:9)

Long ago, there was a certain Buddhist monk, a person of distinction, who fell in love with a court lady of royal birth. When he could no longer restrain himself, he spoke to her and told her of the depth of his emotion. After hesitating for a moment, she said, "There's no reason to be so deeply troubled. I will be leaving court and returning to my home soon, and I will be sure to let you know when I do so." The monk had at first thought of it as perhaps no more than a passing fancy, but, having confessed his love, he now felt more strongly drawn to the woman than ever.

Shortly after, the lady sent word that she had left the court and returned to her home. "Tonight I will be at such-and-such a place," she said. The monk accordingly made his preparations and set off to meet her there.

When he met her, she said, "I have arranged to meet you here because the matter we have to discuss is of such gravity. This body of mine is a thing putrid and rotten beyond description. My head is filled to overflowing with brain matter and other fluids; my skin is stuffed with flesh and bones. Blood flows from my body; pus oozes out—there's nothing here you would want to come close to for an instant. Such being the case, I borrow various external substances to perfume my body and make it more seemly, so it will somehow appear attractive. But if you were to see my true form, you would most certainly find it frightening and repulsive!"

When she had finished explaining all this, she called out to a servant, "Someone there—bring a light!" And a torch was brought, burning brightly in its stand. Then she threw back the curtains that had been hiding her from the monk. "Well then—," she said as she stepped forward. "Can you bear to look at me now?"

Her hair stood up in a mass of tangles like that of a demon. Her face, once so refined, had blue and yellow blotches on it; her feet, no longer their former color, were dirty and unsightly. Blood stained her garments here and there, and they gave off a foul odor that was all but unbearable. Tears pouring down her face, she approached the monk. "If I were to put aside the arts with which I daily adorn myself and appear before you in my true form, this is what my body and my robes would look like, would they not? You are well versed in the Way of the Buddha. So, rather than try to deceive you with feigned appearances, I have ventured, difficult as it is for me, to confront you in my real form!" This was how she explained her actions.

The monk was at a loss for words. Then, weeping profusely, he said, "I have met someone who is a true friend and guide! I will try from now on to turn my mind to worthier thoughts." Then he hurriedly got into his carriage and made his way home.

A Collection of Things Written and Heard in the Past and Present (*Kokon chomonjū*, 1254), the second best known *setsuwa* collection of the Kamakura period (1183–1333) after *A Collection of Tales from Uji* (*Uji shūi monogatari*, early thirteenth century), was edited by Tachibana Narisue. The collection consists of twenty volumes divided into thirty sections, with a total of 697 stories. The thirty sections, each of which begins with an explanation, cover a variety of topics: Shinto (1), Buddhism (2), government and faithful ministers (3), court matters (4), Chinese literature (5), Japanese poetry (6), music, song, and dance (7), calligraphy (8), divinatory practice (9), filial piety (10), amorous affairs (11), martial arts (12), archery (13), horseback riding (14), sumo wrestlers and strong people (15), painting (16), *kemari*, a kind of football (17), gambling (18), thievery (19), celebration (20), laments (21), excursions (22), obsessions (23), fights (24), witty repartee (25), strange events (26), changelings (27), food and drink (28), plants and trees (29), and fish, insects, and animals (30). This *setsuwa* collection, which reveals a strong nostalgia for Heian court culture, tries to give an encyclopedic view of aristocratic society, but at the same time, it reaches beyond that, particularly in the second half, to examine various aspects of commoner life in the Kamakura period. One of the characteristics of a *Kokon chomonjū* anecdote is the twist at the end.

Section 15, on sumo wrestlers and strong people, extends from sumo wrestlers in the imperial palace to physically strong individuals in the world of commoners. Two of the more interesting stories, including "How Saeki Ujinaga Met Ooiko, a Very Strong Woman of Takashima, and of Ooiko's Earlier Display of Great Strength in Water Disputes" (15:377), are about strong women. One of the compelling stories in section 18, on gambling, is "How a Samurai Who Served Lord Kazan'in Tadatsune, Minister of the Right, Won at Gambling and Received the Tonsure Thanks to His Wife" (18:423). Section 30, on fish, insects, and animals, contains the tale "How a Man Called Umanojō Shot a Male Mandarin Duck in Akanuma in Michinoku Province and Then Received the Tonsure" (30:713), which reveals the confluence of the tradition of the *monogatari* (court tale) with the realities of provincial hunting.

How Saeki Ujinaga Met Ooiko, a Very Strong Woman of Takashima, and of Ooiko's Earlier Display of Great Strength in Water Disputes (15:377)

When Saeki Ujinaga, traveling from Echizen Province, first set out to join the sumo tournament meeting in Kyoto, he passed through the village of Ishibashi in Takashima County in Ōmi Province. There he saw a beautiful woman dipping water from a river with a pail and carrying it on her head. One glimpse of her stirred his heart, and, certain that he could not simply pass her by, he got off his horse and slipped his hand beside her arm that was holding the pail.

The woman smiled but showed no sign of resenting his action or loosening her grip on the pail. Finding this particularly appealing, he pushed in his arm firmly next to hers, whereupon she shifted the pail to the other hand and clamped down tightly on Ujinaga's arm. Ujinaga found this even more engaging, but although the time passed, he discovered that he could not get his arm free. When he tried to pull away, she only clamped harder, so he could not possibly free his arm. In the end, he had no other option than to keep on walking beside her.

When they arrived at her house, they went in, and, after placing the pail on the floor, she loosened her grip on his arm. Laughing, she said, "Still, what kind of man are you, that you play a trick like this on me?" She seemed to be saying that he should have known better, which confused him completely.

"I am from the province of Echigo and am on my way to the sumo tournament in Kyoto," said Ujinaga. "There are bound to be strong men from all the various provinces taking part."

When the woman heard this, she agreed. "You're right—there will be. It's a tricky situation. The capital is large, and there are certain to be many men of great strength, the kind who stand out in the world. I'm not saying that you're a complete nobody, but you don't have the power for such a demanding role either, and that's the kind you're likely to find yourself up against. Let me see—how much time is there before the tournament? You've got three times seven days. That gives us a little time," she said.

So they proceeded slowly, not hurrying, taking their time, following the woman's directions. Beginning on the first evening, she fixed rice that was harder to chew than usual. She herself did the cooking, so you couldn't tell that it was not ordinary rice. For the first seven evenings, it was indistinguishable from regular rice. For the next seven evenings, it became increasingly hard. And by the last seven evenings, he was completely used to it. Thus, over the course of three times seven, she skillfully accustomed him to the diet he would face. "Now hurry on your way to the tournament!" she said. "I don't think you're likely to run into trouble!" And off he went. It was a strange encounter indeed!

Now this Ooiko of Takashima was very active in matters pertaining to the rice fields. When it came time to draw water into the fields, disputes over the use of water often arose, quarrels about whether the water should go this way or that. And when Ooiko did not think that the water had been distributed equitably, she took a stone, square in shape and six or seven *shaku*[1] to a side, and, acting under cover of darkness, put it over the hole where the water came in, so it blocked the water to the others' fields and allowed it to flow only into hers. Thus she ensured her own plentiful supply of water, while making sure that nobody else had any.

The next morning, when the village people looked, they were astounded at what they found. They saw that the stone diverting the water was one that a hundred of them could not move.

---

1. A *shaku*, a unit of length, is just short of one foot.

Eventually, the other villagers, admitting defeat, said, "All right—we give up! But from today, when water is needed, let it flow as before. Please move the stone." "All right!" she replied, and when night came, she moved the stone away. Thereafter, there were no more disputes in the village, but neither did the fields dry up. This came about because of the great strength of this girl Ooiko.

The stone came to be known as Ooiko's Outlet Stone and is preserved in the county.

How a Samurai Who Served Lord Kazan'in Tadatsune, Minister of the Right, Won at Gambling and Received the Tonsure Thanks to His Wife (18:423)

When Lord Kazan'in, Minister of the Right,[2] was in power, the samurai in his service loved the kind of gambling known as *shichihan*,[3] playing it day and night. No matter how much the Minister of the Right inveighed against it, he could not stop them.

There was one samurai who was very poor and hence was not included in those who played *shichihan*. His wife was in the service of the Court Counsellor Fujiwara no Sadatoshi and each evening went to Ninna-ji to work.[4]

One night, this samurai was spending the night with his wife. But, heaving a long sigh, he could not get to sleep and passed the whole time lost in thought. His wife, wondering, asked him the reason. "It's nothing important," he told her. "Just that I think of how poor I am, and I can't seem to get sleepy."

She did not believe him, however, and pressed for a more concrete answer. At last he said, "It isn't really anything. But it irks me to think that

2. The Minister of the Right was Fujiwara no Tadatsune (1173–1229).
3. *Shichihan* was a gambling game played with dice.
4. In 1201, Fujiwara no Sadayoshi (1148–1209) retired to the Buddhist temple of Ninna-ji and took the tonsure.

all the men in Lord Kazan'in's service, young and old alike, are playing that game every day. I'm one of that group, but because I haven't a penny to spare, I can't join them. I suppose I'll always be poor like this, and it's not that I want to be able to gamble. But I see them having all that fun, and I think that I alone can't take part in it and join the others. And it's not just about gambling—it's about other things too. I begin to wonder what I'm doing with my life."

When he had gone this far, his wife expressed her sympathy. "I understand—it's just as you say. When you're dealing with others, there are good times and bad times, but to be left out of everything—that's hard to take. But wait until the night is over. I think perhaps I can help," she said.

"At least you understand," he replied. "Most women, whatever the circumstances, if they hear that one word 'gambling,' they fly up in the air! I'm thankful that you're not like that. But actually I'm not very eager to take up gambling, though I appreciate your encouragement. I really do."

"You don't have to thank me," said his wife. "The night will soon be over."

And when it was over, she slipped out of her lone robe and exchanged it for five hundred *mon*.[5] Giving this money to her husband, she said, "Take this and gamble to your heart's content! Whether you bet with ten or twenty *kan*[6] or with just a little sum, the pleasure is the same, isn't it? And you've said you don't care that much about the size of the bet."

The man took the money with many thanks, and the following morning, with the money stored in his breast, hurried to the hall of Lord Kazan'in. There he joined the throng who were milling about.

"I've never done this before," he thought to himself. "Although I've watched them doing it morning and night, I've never taken part. I don't know how the dice will roll—I'd better ask somebody." He addressed one of the gamblers, asking if he could play.

"With all of us playing, is this fellow going to hold back? Is he some kind of goody-goody who doesn't gamble? What's going on?" said the man.

5. The *mon* was a coin of small value that had a hole in it and was customarily strung on a string.
6. The *kan* was a unit of currency, a sum equal to a thousand *mon*.

"Oh, don't say that! From today on, I'd like to join in," he replied.

He had only a small sum of money to bet, and he thought that if he tried to use it a little bit at a time, it would be no good. So he decided to put all of it out at once—"and if I lose, then I lose!" he thought.

When the others had finished laying their bets, the result was announced. It was all over, and he had won one *kan*. "I didn't even know what was going on the first time, and they're going to do it again!" he thought. They were doing it again, so he put down the one *kan*.

Once again he had won—and he now had two *kan*.

Then he thought, "I'd better put aside five hundred *mon* so I won't lose that—I'll return that to my wife." He put the five hundred *mon* in the breast of his robe and bet the remaining one *kan* and five hundred *mon*. "I'll do it my way this time," he thought—and again he had won, three *kan* this time.

He went on in this way—one *kan*, two *kan*—one good bet after another, until he had reached the total of thirty *kan* or more. "That's enough of big winning!" he thought to himself. "Let's stop here." And he withdrew from the game with over thirty *kan*. "What are you quitting now for?" exclaimed the others in surprise. But all he said was, "Enough for now—I'll go on another time."

That night, the samurai sent someone to Ninna-ji to take his wife her money. The next day, he and his wife spent the whole day making plans, going about it in a very deliberate manner. They purchased two or three new chests for clothing and other belongings, which gave off a sparkle of opulence, and in the early morning of the second day, he had them brought to the Kazan'in residence.

Then he wrote out a Vow of Intention and posted it on a pillar in the office of the samurai. The Vow of Intention stated: "From this day forward, I vow never to gamble. In the past, I once did so, joining with the others, but that was only once. From now on, if I ever do so again, may I be punished in this life and the next." When he had posted it, some of his companions condemned him as a cheap spoilsport, but others praised him.

The man then went to his wife's place and announced, "I now have thirty *kan*. I'm giving you ten *kan* as your share. I ought by rights give you the whole thing, since if it hadn't been for your kindness, there wouldn't be anything at all. However, I'm getting along in years and probably don't have a great many left. I intend to enter the priesthood if I can, but I don't have any money saved up to cover my meals. So that's a problem. But if I set aside the remaining twenty *kan* for my meals, and chant Amida Buddha's name, I think I might make it to the Pure Land. I'll never forget how kind you've been all these years. And, unless it's repugnant to you, we can still meet from time to time. Perhaps you could even wash up the old rags I'll be wearing. That would be nice, too."

"Let me congratulate you on your decision to take religious vows," said his wife. "It's true—this world we live in is an uncertain place. And that you see it that way makes me happy, not only for your sake but for mine, too."

Having received his wife's approval of his plan, he was delighted and at once took religious vows. Then, taking ten *kan* of the original thirty *kan*, he proceeded to the Shijō area of the city. There, in a very small house, he said to the owner, "Here is ten *kan*, which I would like to give you. In the space of a month, I will be spending the first fifteen days in your house. The money is to pay for the two meals that I will eat on such days. When the money runs out, that will be the end of the arrangement." The master of the house agreed to the conditions, and so the matter was settled.

"You may think," he said, "that if one does business in this fashion, the house would be too small, so how could being cramped up in such a small room be all right? But it's just a matter of attitude." He was in fact quite content with his room under the eaves. And from there he looked down on the people of the world dashing around and realized how vain and impermanent it all was. And so he intoned the Buddha's name and passed his first fifteen-day period. And then he took his last ten *kan*, went to the Shichijō area of the city, and made a similar arrangement for his meals in the latter fifteen-day period of the month.

As the merit of his invocation of the Buddha's name piled up and his devotion to the Way became apparent, those around him were affected, large numbers of them turning to religion. One after another they came forward, insisting that his meal that day would be their contribution. Thus his ten *kan* was no longer needed at either house, and the masters of the two places benefited accordingly.

When the time came for him to die, he knew in advance what was ahead. He journeyed to his wife's place in Ninna-ji, where without the slightest difficulty, in full possession of his faculties, he sat down in the correct posture, put his palms together, and, raising his voice, recited the Buddha's name and passed away. And through the power of his excellent example, his wife, too, became an ardent proponent of the faith, all through the beneficent guidance of the Buddha Amida.

How a Man Called Umanojō Shot a Male Mandarin Duck in Akanuma in Michinoku Province and Then Received the Tonsure (30:713)

In Michinoku Province, the village of Tamura, there lived a man named Umanojō So-and-so who raised hawks. One day, when his hawks had failed to catch any birds and he was coming home empty-handed, at a place called Akanuma he saw a pair of mandarin ducks flying about. Fitting an arrow with a special type of point to his bow, he shot and killed the male of the pair. He fed the body to his hawks and put the remainder in his bag and took it home.

That night in a dream, a beautiful little woman came to his pillow, crying piteously. Wondering at this, he asked, "Who are you, and why are you crying?"

She replied, "Yesterday at Akanuma, a terrible thing happened. You killed my husband, my companion of many years, and therefore I weep in unbearable sorrow. I have come to tell you of this. Because of this sorrow, I do not know how I can go on living." Weeping uncontrollably, she recited this poem in Japanese and then went away, still weeping:

Hi kurureba	As evening comes,
sasoi shi mono wo	how sad that I,
Akanuma no	who had slept with my mate,
makomo-gakure no	must sleep alone in the shade
hitorine zo uki	of the marsh grass of Akanuma.

Shocked and saddened by these words, on the following day the man opened his bag to find the bill of the female bird paired with that of her mate. Because of what had happened, he abandoned his regular occupation and took the tonsure. He was a samurai in the service of Lord Nakayoshi, former commissioner of the Ministry of Justice.

TALES OF RENUNCIATION

SENJŪSHŌ

Tales of Renunciation (*Senjūshō*, late thirteenth century) is a collection of 121 Buddhist *setsuwa* divided into nine books. Although the date of 1183 is given in its colophon, it probably was composed about a century later. The collection has been popularly attributed to Saigyō (1118–1190), a noted monk and *waka* (classical poetry) poet of the late Heian period (794–1185), probably because Saigyō figures prominently in the collection. He appears as the first-person narrator in one of the tales, and poems from *Collection of a Mountain Home* (*Sankashū*, 1180), Saigyō's poetry collection, are incorporated into several tales, whereas several other tales appear to be based on head notes from *Sankashū*. But it is clear that Saigyō was not the author or compiler.

The *Senjūshō* is unified by the theme of renunciation. The tales usually begin with an anecdote, followed by an exposition or a commentary on the main theme of the anecdote. The first tale in *Senjūshō*, "The Venerable Zōga" (1:1), is representative of the format of the stories. The commentary, which is almost as long as the anecdote itself, argues that attachment to worldly possessions and reputation leads to sin and must be overcome, which Zōga does in an extreme fashion. Significantly, the eccentric Zōga is inspired by Amaterasu, the Sun Goddess, whose presence reflects the Shinto–Buddhist syncretism typical of the medieval period. The story "The Woman of Pleasure at Eguchi" (9:8), which recounts Saigyō's encounter with a prostitute, is the most famous of the Saigyō episodes and was the source for the *nō* play *Eguchi*.

❋

The Venerable Zōga (1:1)

Long ago, there was a man called the Venerable Zōga.[1] From a very early age, he longed to attain enlightenment, and he spent a thousand nights cloistered in the Konponchūdō, the main hall of the Tendai headquarters on Mount Hiei. There he prayed earnestly, but somehow still could not seem to acquire the true determination needed to pursue the search for enlightenment.

Once he went alone on a pilgrimage to the Grand Shrine in Ise.[2] There it was revealed to him in a dream that if he wished to gain the true determination for enlightenment, he must learn to look on this body of his as not a body at all. On receiving this revelation, he was much startled and concluded that it meant he must cast aside all desire for fame and gain. "Very well," he told himself, "I will cast them aside!" With that, he took off all his priestly robes and gave them away to the beggars. He proceeded in this fashion until he had given away even his unlined under robe, and he left the shrine in a state of total nakedness.

The people who saw him gathered around, thinking that he had gone mad to behave in such a strange and unsightly manner. He paid not the slightest attention to them, however, but went on his way, begging as he did so.

After four days, he returned to the place where he had lived formerly on Mount Hiei and entered the quarters of his mentor, the Great Teacher Jie.[3]

1. The Venerable Zōga (917–1003) was the son of Tachibana no Tsunehira, the "court consultant" mentioned later in the tale. He studied to become a monk at Enryaku-ji, the head temple of the Tendai school on Mount Hiei, and later retired to Tōnomine, a mountain south of Nara.
2. The famous Grand Shrine in Ise was dedicated to Amaterasu, the Sun Goddess. That Zōga, a Buddhist monk, would pray at the leading Shinto shrine indicates the degree to which the two religions were intertwined in this period of Japanese history.
3. The Great Teacher Jie was the renowned Tendai monk and scholar Ryōgen (912–985).

The Venerable Zōga walks after having discarded his clothes. (From an Edo-period wood-block edition of *Senjūshō*, with the permission of Komine Kazuaki)

Some of his fellow monks supposed that this man, a court consultant's son, had gone out of his mind, while others were embarrassed even to look at him. The Great Teacher Jie, summoning him into his presence, acknowledged that he had understood the importance of rejecting fame and gain. But he cautioned him that there was no need to go to such extremes. "Just behave in a respectable manner and banish from your mind all thoughts of fame and gain!" he said.

"But this is precisely the way someone who has long ago cast aside fame and gain ought to behave!" said Zōga. Then, exclaiming, "Oh, oh, what happiness is mine!" he rushed out of the room. The Great Teacher Jie followed him out beyond the gate, where, the tears flowing helplessly from his eyes, he stood and watched as Zōga went on his way.

In the end, Zōga wandered about until he reached Mount Tōnomine, in Yamato Province, where he settled in the spot where the Meditation Master Chirō had had his hermitage.

Truly there is nothing more reprehensible than the desire for fame and gain, or the ills that arise from the three poisons of greed, anger, and ignorance. Because we believe that this body of ours really exists, we devise all kinds of measures to help it along. Men born into warrior families will draw the arrows from their quivers, brandish their three-foot swords, and risk their lives in battle, though it may mean death, all for the sake of fame and gain and mastery over others. Women will paint their willow-leaf eyebrows in thin lines of mascara and scent their garments with orchid and musk, hoping to drive away every trace of love's fickleness, and this, too, they do only because of their desire for fame and gain.

And, again, when people don the black-dyed robes of clerics and twirl their rosaries in their hands, it is all done simply because they calculate that they can win others over to their faith and thus earn their living in the world. Or when they strive for high position or high office, hoping that they may take part in the Buddhist ceremonies of the noble families and be attended by three thousand monk disciples, it is because they cannot get fame and gain out of their minds.

Such, it goes without saying, are those who do not understand the facts. But those who have had their eyes opened by the Yuishiki or Shikan teachings[4] and who can comprehend the highest principles expounded in the Buddhist scriptures still fail to cast aside fame and gain, but go on dwelling in the sea of birth and death.

Anyone who has tried to reform these habits of mind that have been with one through lifetime after lifetime knows how difficult that can be. And yet this Venerable Zōga was able in an instant to divest himself of thoughts of fame and gain. Was that not an admirable feat?

If he had not had divine assistance from the Grand Shrine in Ise, however, how could he have driven such thoughts from his mind? He swept away the massive clouds of greed, anger, and ignorance; washed himself clean of the perpetual darkness of fame and gain in the waters of the Isuzu River;[5] and through the holy light of the great goddess Amaterasu rid himself of it. This was a most wonderful and auspicious affair, one that, whatever the age, should never be forgotten!

The Woman of Pleasure at Eguchi (9:8)

Some time ago, around the twentieth day of the Ninth Month, I passed by a place called Eguchi. I could see the houses crowded together along the riverbanks to the north and south, lodgings of harlots hoping to cater to travelers on the boats passing up and down the river. As I was gazing at them and thinking what a pitiful sight they were, a sudden icy shower, impatient for the start of winter, began drenching down. I approached one of the houses, an odd and dilapidated affair, and asked if I could beg lodging until the rain let up. But the "woman of pleasure" who presided over the house showed no inclination to heed my request. On the spur of the moment, I recited this poem:

4. The Yuishiki, or Conscious-Only, teachings are those of the Shingon school of Buddhism; the Shikan, or Concentration and Insight, teachings are those of the Tendai school. Both were taught in the temple of Mount Hiei, where Zōga studied.
5. The Isuzu is the small river that runs through the Grand Shrine in Ise.

Yo no naka o	It's hard to despise
itou made koso	the whole world
katakarame	as a borrowed lodging,
kari no yado o	but that you should begrudge me
oshimu kimi kana	even a brief stay!

The woman of the house, smiling a little, replied with this poem:

Ie o izuru	Because I heard you were someone
hito to shi kikeba	who had left the household life,
kari no yado	my only thought was to warn you:
kokoro tomu na to	don't let your mind dwell
omou bakari zo	on this borrowed lodging!

Then she quickly ushered me in. I had intended to stay only until the shower was over, but her poem was so interesting that I ended up spending the entire night.

The woman of the house was at that time something over forty, highly refined in both appearance and manner. We spent the whole night talking of nothing in particular, and she said to me, "I have been a prostitute since the time I was very young. But although for years I have carried on in this fashion, it has always been profoundly distasteful to me. Women, they say, are deeply sinful in nature. But to have to live the life of a harlot—it must surely be due to some fault that I committed in a previous existence. How hateful it is! These past two or three years, I've come to deeply regret such conduct, and since I'm well along in years, I no longer follow those ways.

"Although they are the same bells from the temple in the fields that I always hear, when evening comes they seem to me so sad that before I know it, I give way to tears. This life, brief as it is—must it always be as drab and meaningless as this? Then, when dawn comes, my mind clears a little, and when I hear the birds taking fond leave of one another, I am struck even more by the sadness of things.

"At evening, I wonder how I will fare when the night is over. When dawn comes, I ponder whether, now that the night is over, I should not make up my mind to become a nun. But so many long months and years

I've lived in the world in this fashion that I'm like the cuckoo of the Himalaya Mountains.[6] And so, regrettable as it is, I have yet to take that step!" Her voice trailed off in sobs.

Listening to her, I found her words so pitiful, and so filled with meaning, that the sleeves of my black monk's robe were drenched with tears. When morning came, we took leave of each other, promising at a future time to meet again.

During my return trip, I recalled her with admiration, the tears again and again springing to my eyes. Even now, she remains in my thoughts, and just the sight of grass or trees will often stir deep memories of her. When people speak of how "wild words and fancy phrases" can lead one to praise the Buddhist doctrines, this must be what they mean.[7] If I had not recited my poem, inept as it was, with the words "that you should begrudge me / even a brief stay!" she would not have granted me lodging. And then how would I have ever come to know this remarkable person? It was all because of "you," I keep remembering with joy, that I was able, for a moment at least, to glimpse within my heart and mind the seeds of unsurpassed enlightenment.

The month when we had promised to meet again arrived, and I thought of visiting her. But an important personage came from the capital, disrupting my schedule, and I was unable to carry out my plan.

However, I found someone who was traveling in her direction and was able to send word by him, entrusting him with a poem that read:

6. According to Buddhist lore, the cuckoo of the Himalayas is a foolish bird that, having failed to provide itself with adequate protection against the cold, shivers all night, vowing to build a proper nest the next morning. But with the warmth of dawn, all its good intentions are forgotten.

7. The phrase "wild words and fancy phrases" (*kyōgen kigo*) derives from a piece written by the Chinese poet Bo Juyi (772–846) when he deposited a copy of his writings in a Buddhist temple in Luoyang. In it, he expressed a wish that "these worldly literary labors of my present existence, these transgressions of wild words and fancy phrases," might be transformed into causes for deeper religious understanding. But many Buddhists felt that undue attention to poetry and other types of secular literature was in fact an impediment to such understanding.

Karisome no	Don't let your thoughts dwell
yo ni wa omoi o	on this fleeting world!—
nokosu na to	those words
kikishi koto no ha	you spoke to me
wasurare mo sezu	I've not forgotten.

She sent her answer back by the same messenger. I hurried to open it, and found these words written in a beautiful hand:

Wasurezu to	Not forgotten—no sooner
mazu kiku kara ni	had I heard those words
sode nurete	than tears wet my sleeve.
waga mi wa itou	I too have come to hate
yume no yo no naka	this world of dreams.

And at the end she added, "I have changed my garb for that of a nun, but my thoughts have yet to go along!" And she enclosed this poem:

Kami oroshi	I've shaved my head,
koromo no iro wa	my robes
somenuru ni	are now dyed black,
nao tsurenaki wa	but my thoughts
kokoro nari keri	fail to make the change.

Once again, I found myself deeply moved, the tears drenching my sleeves. What an admirable person, this "woman of pleasure"!

Women of her type who make their living in that way hope, it seems, to find someone suitable who will love and look after them. But this woman put such hopes aside and thought only of what awaited her in her next existence. A rare case, is she not? Surely she must have performed more than her share of religious acts in her previous existences. And the seeds of those virtuous deeds that she planted in one lifetime after another were then brought to fruition by the waters of the river at Eguchi.

Even her poems are interesting. And when she said to me, "At evening, I wonder how I will fare when the night is over," or "When dawn comes, my tears flow"—did she remain to the end in this questioning frame of mind? But no, she became a nun.

After that, I hoped to pay her a visit, but I heard that she was no longer living in Eguchi, and so those plans came to nothing. Again and again, I find myself wondering what sort of end came to that "woman of pleasure."

Collection of Sand and Pebbles (*Shasekishū*, 1279–1283) consists of ten books. After editing the collection, Priest Mujū (1226–1312) revised and rewrote a number of the *setsuwa*, often with the intention of making difficult Buddhist doctrine easier to understand. Some of the *setsuwa* are stories about everyday life, with humor, wordplay, and comic twists at the end. Indeed, the collection greatly influenced later fiction, particularly the *hanashi-bon* (humorous books), *kana-zōshi* (*kana* booklets), and *ukiyo-zōshi* (books of the floating world) genres of the Edo period (1600–1867), when the text was reprinted many times.

The *Shasekishū* differs from other *setsuwa* collections in that the individual stories are used to advance Mujū's own arguments and to explain complex Buddhist issues. He uses metaphors, cites sources, and alludes to other texts, making the collection more like a vernacular Buddhist treatise (*hōgo*). But Mujū also was interested in *monogatari* (court tales), which is evident in his writing and in his treatment of salvation and fiction writing. Both "The Scholar Who Loved Poetry" (5:11) and "The Deep Meaning Underlying the Way of Japanese Poetry" (5:12) encapsulate Mujū's views on this complex subject.

Conventional morality held that *kyōgen kigo* (wild words and fancy phrases) could lead to sin, attachment, immoral conduct, and corruption. The prevailing Buddhist view was that both the composition and the appreciation of fiction and poetry were to be avoided as impediments to enlightenment, but Mujū argues that "wild words and fancy phrases" could serve as a vehicle for achieving Buddhist awakening (nirvana) in this world, as an expedient means to a higher end. That is, poetry may lead us to a deeper understanding of the impermanence of the world or to a better appreciation of the Pure Land, the Western Paradise.

This function of literature as an expedient (*hōben*) was even more true for *waka* (classical poetry), which Mujū regarded as a means of meditation, particularly in the form of *dharani*, mystic verses that served to establish rapport with the divine. In *Shasekishū*, Mujū introduces the issue of *honji suijaku* (original ground–manifest traces), with Shinto deities in Japan seen as manifest traces of the Buddhist gods, who originated in India. The native Shinto gods composed *waka*, regarded as the manifestations of the Indian-derived *dharani*, which enable the chanter to become one with the Buddha.

The Scholar Who Loved Poetry (5:11)

In his studies, the Supervisor of Priests Eshin[1] paid no attention to other disciplines but was wholly concerned with matters pertaining to the religious mind. He therefore had great disdain for trivial concerns such as those commonly referred to as "wild words and fancy phrases."[2]

Among his disciples was a young boy who day and night devoted his thoughts to the composition of Japanese poetry. His fellow disciples several times reported on the matter, saying, "Students are naturally expected to spend all their time on their studies. But this boy is quite hopeless and cares for nothing but poetry. One like that can set a bad example for the

---

1. Eshin (942–1017), better known by the name Genshin, was an eminent priest and scholar of Enryaku-ji temple on Mount Hiei and the author of *The Essentials of Salvation* (*Ōjōyōshū*, 985), a highly influential Buddhist text.
2. The phrase "wild words and fancy phrases" (*kyōgen kigo*) derives from a piece written by the Chinese poet Bo Juyi (772–846) when he deposited a copy of his writings in a Buddhist temple in Luoyang. In it, he expressed a wish that "these worldly literary labors of my present existence, these transgressions of wild words and fancy phrases," might be transformed into causes for deeper religious understanding. But many Buddhists felt that undue attention to poetry and other types of secular literature was in fact an impediment to such understanding.

others. Under the circumstances, he had best be sent back to his home village tomorrow."

The boy, however, was quite unaware of what was being said about him. Once, when the moon shone and all was quiet, he went out on the veranda and, as the night deepened, cupped his hands as though dipping up water and recited this poem:

Te ni musubu	This image of the moon
mizu ni yadoreru	lodged in the water
tsuki kage wa	I hold in my hand—
aru ka naki ka	and this world we live in as well—
yo no mo sumu kana	are they real, or are they not?

When Eshin heard this, he immediately said, "The poem is deeply moving in both its form and its meaning!" He therefore let the boy remain among his disciples and himself became fond of poetry, many of his poems being preserved in the anthologies compiled in later ages.

It is also reported that the boy, observing a boat on Lake Biwa in Ōmi, recited this poem:

Yo no naka o	This worlds of ours—
nani ni tatoen	what to compare it to?
asaborake	White waves
kogiyuku fune no	in the wake of a boat
ato no shiranami	rowing away at dawn.

In this way, we are told, Eshin came to love poetry. The first poem the boy recited was by Tsurayuki, written when he was gravely ill and hoped thereby to ease his mind. The second poem was by Mansei.[3] The boy

---

3. Ki no Tsurayuki (868–945) was a renowned poet and an editor of the *Kokinshū* (*Collection of Ancient and Modern Japanese Poems*, ca. 905). Sami Mansei (dates unknown) was a poet of the mid-Nara period (710–784). The boy quotes a slightly revised version of Mansei's poem.

recited these poems on occasions that were appropriate to them. Both are preserved in the *Shūi wakashū*.[4] Eshin himself composed the following poem:

Urayamashi	Enviable!
ikanaru sora no	How the moon,
tsuki nareba	whatever sky it's in,
kokoro no mama ni	never wavers in its goal,
nishi ni yukuran	moving ever westward![5]

The term "wild words and fancy phrases," when applied to Japanese poetry, refers to poetry that is defiled, because such poetry is bound up with emotional attachments, colored by improper feelings, and decked out in empty words. But when poetry accords with the principles of the sacred teachings, wakens in our minds a sense of impermanence, and turns us away from worldly concerns, crass thoughts, and all craving for fame and profit—as when we observe the falling leaves and sense the ephemerality of this world, or when, by writing of snow or the moon, we convey to others the inherent purity of the mind—then it may guide us into the Way of the Buddha and aid us to understand its doctrines. Therefore, when persons of past times practiced the teachings of the Buddha, they did not necessarily reject the study of Japanese poetry entirely.

Hence we find that, when the occasion arose to express their feelings, such persons often wrote Japanese poems. For example, at a gathering attended by the venerable priest of Ōhara, Priest Saigyō,[6] and others, Eshin himself, writing on the subject of old age, composed this poem:

---

4. The *Shūi wakashū* (*Gleanings Collection of Japanese Poetry*, 1005–1007), often abbreviated as *Shūishū*, is the third imperial anthology of Japanese poetry.
5. West in Buddhist terms is the direction of Amida Buddha's Western Paradise.
6. The "venerable priest of Ōhara" is Jakuren (d. 1202), a late Heian poet; Saigyō (1118–1190) is among the most famous of early Japanese poets.

Yama no ha ni	As their shapes sink
kage katabukite	beyond the leaves of the mountain rim,
kuyashiki ya	how I grieve at
munashiku sugishi	the empty passing
tsuki hi narikeri	of these suns and moons!

Listening to the poem many ages after, if we stop to consider the writer's feelings, we realize that even a man who had freed himself from emotional entanglements was still conscious of the sadness of things.

The Deep Meaning Underlying the Way of Japanese Poetry (5:12)

When we come to fully understand Japanese poetry [*waka*], we can see that it has the virtue of curbing thoughts that are disordered, coarse, and turbulent and of achieving a state of calm and serenity. Employing few words, it conveys vast meaning. It has the virtue of *sōji*, or all-encompassing mystic utterances. A *sōji* is a *dhārani*.[7]

The gods of our land of Japan are local manifestations of the Buddhas and bodhisattvas, the greatest of which is the manifested body of the Buddha.[8] The god Susano-o initiated the practice of Japanese poetry with his poem in thirty-one syllables on "Izumo where eight clouds rise."[9] His poem is, in effect, no different from the words of the Buddha. The *dhārani* of India, like Susano-o's poem, are couched in the language of the country to which they are addressed. The Buddha employed the language of India to convey his mystic utterances.

---

7. *Dhārani* are spells or mystic formulas used in Buddhism. *Sōji*, a translation of the Sanskrit word *dhārani*, means "all-retaining," because one who recites a *dhārani* is able to remember all of the Buddha's teachings.

8. One of the three bodies of a Buddha, this is the one in which he manifests himself in the temporal world.

9. In "Izumo where eight clouds rise," the first poem in the *Record of Ancient Matters* (*Kojiki*, 712), Susano-o describes an eightfold fence that he has built in Izumo to protect his wife.

Therefore, the Meditation Master Yixing, in his *Annotations on the Mahāvairochana Sutra*, says: "The local languages of the various regions are all *dhāraṇi*."[10] If the Buddha had appeared in our land of Japan, he would simply have used the language of Japan in which to express his mystic utterances.

10. *Annotations on the Mahāvairochana Sutra* (*Great Sun Sutra*; Ch. *Darijing*, Jp. *Dainichi-kyō*) is a compilation of the lectures of Shanwuwei (Skt. Shubhākarasimha, 637–735) on the sutra made by his disciple Yixing (683–727).

BIBLIOGRAPHY OF TRANSLATIONS AND
STUDIES IN WESTERN LANGUAGES

TRANSLATIONS

Backus, Robert L., trans. *The Riverside Counselor's Stories: Vernacular Fiction of Late Heian Japan*. Stanford, Calif.: Stanford University Press, 1985.

Brower, Robert H. "The *Konzyaku monogatarisyū*: An Historical and Critical Introduction, with Annotated Translations of Seventy-eight Tales." Ph.D. diss., University of Michigan, 1952.

Brownlee, John, trans. "*Jikkinshō*: A Miscellany of Ten Maxims." *Monumenta Nipponica* 29, no. 2 (1974): 121–161.

Chingen. *Miraculous Tales of the Lotus Sutra from Ancient Japan: The Dainihonkoku Hokekyōkenki of Prince Chingen*. Translated and annotated by Yoshiko Kurata Dykstra. Hirakata City, Osaka: Intercultural Research Institute, Kansai University of Foreign Studies, 1983.

Dykstra, Yoshiko Kurata, trans. "Jizō, the Most Merciful: Tales from *Jizō Bosatsu reigenki*." *Monumenta Nipponica* 33, no. 2 (1978): 179–200.

——, trans. *The Konjaku Tales: Chinese Section: From a Medieval Japanese Collection*. Hirakata City, Osaka: Intercultural Research Institute, Kansai University of Foreign Studies, 1994.

——, trans. *The Konjaku Tales: Indian Section: From a Medieval Japanese Collection*. Hirakata City, Osaka: Intercultural Research Institute, Kansai University of Foreign Studies, 1986.

——, trans. *The Konjaku Tales: Japanese Section: From a Medieval Japanese Collection*. 3 vols. Hirakata City, Osaka: Intercultural Research Institute, Kansai University of Foreign Studies, 1998, 2001, 2003.

——, trans. "Notable Tales Old and New: Tachibana Narisue's *Kokon Chomonjū*." *Monumenta Nipponica* 47, no. 4 (1992): 469–493.

——, trans. "Tales of the Compassionate Kannon: The *Hasedera Kannon genki.*" *Monumenta Nipponica* 31, no. 2 (1976): 113–143.

Forster, John S., trans. "*Uji shūi monogatari*: Selected Translation." *Monumenta Nipponica* 20, nos. 1–2 (1965): 135–208.

Frank, Bernard, trans. *Histoires qui sont maintenant du passé.* Paris: Gallimard, 1968.

Geddes, Ward, trans. *Kara monogatari: Tales of China.* Tempe: Center for Asian Studies, Arizona State University, 1984.

Jones, S. W., trans. *Ages Ago: Thirty-seven Tales from the Konjaku monogatari Collection.* Cambridge, Mass.: Harvard University Press, 1959.

Kamens, Edward B. *The Three Jewels: A Study and Translation of Minamoto Tanemori's Sanbōe.* Ann Arbor: Center for Japanese Studies, University of Michigan, 1988.

Keikai. *Miraculous Stories from the Japanese Buddhist Tradition: The Nihon ryōiki of the Monk Kyōkai.* Translated and annotated by Kyoko Motomochi Nakamura. Cambridge, Mass.: Harvard University Press, 1973.

Mills, D. E. *A Collection of Tales from Uji: A Study and Translation of Uji shūi monogatari.* Cambridge: Cambridge University Press, 1970.

Moore, Jean. "*Senjūshō*: Buddhist Tales of Renunciation." *Monumenta Nipponica* 41, no. 2 (1986): 127–174.

Morrell, Robert E. "Mujū Ichien's Shinto–Buddhist Syncretism: *Shasekishū*, Book 1." *Monumenta Nipponica* 28, no. 4 (1973): 447–488.

Mujū, Ichien. *Collection de sable et de pierres: Shasekishū.* Translation, preface, and commentaries by Hartmut O. Rotermund. Paris: Gallimard, 1979.

——. *Sand and Pebbles (Shasekishū): The Tales of Mujū Ichien, a Voice for Pluralism in Kamakura Buddhism.* Translated and edited by Robert E. Morrell. Albany: State University of New York Press, 1985.

Pandey, Rajyashree. "*Suki* and Religious Awakening: Kamo no Chōmei's *Hosshinshū.*" *Monumenta Nipponica* 41, no. 3 (1992): 299–321.

——. "Women, Sexuality, and Enlightenment: *Kankyo no Tomo.*" *Monumenta Nipponica* 50, no. 3 (1995): 325–356.

Philippi, Donald L. "Two Tales from the *Nippon ryōiki.*" *Journal of the Association of Teachers of Japanese* 5 (1960): 53–55.

Shirane, Haruo, ed. *Traditional Japanese Literature: An Anthology, Beginnings to 1600.* New York: Columbia University Press, 2007.

Tahara, Mildred M., trans. *Tales of Yamato: A Tenth-Century Poem-Tale.* Honolulu: University Press of Hawaii, 1980.

Tyler, Royall, trans. *Japanese Tales.* New York: Pantheon, 1987.

Ueda, Akinari. *Tales of Moonlight and Rain*. Translated by Anthony H. Chambers. New York: Columbia University Press, 2007.

Ury, Marian. "*Genkō shakusho*: Japan's First Comprehensive History of Buddhism." Ph.D. diss., University of California at Berkeley, 1971.

——. "Nuns and Other Female Devotees in *Genkō shakusho* (1322), Japan's First History of Buddhism." Revised for publication by Robert Borgen. In *Engendering Faith: Women and Buddhism in Premodern Japan*, edited by Barbara Ruch, 189–207. Ann Arbor: Center for Japanese Studies, University of Michigan, 2002.

——, trans. "The Ōe Conversations." *Monumenta Nipponica* 48, no. 3 (1993): 359–380.

——, trans. "Recluses and Eccentric Monks: Tales from the *Hosshinshū* by Kamo no Chōmei." *Monumenta Nipponica* 27, no. 2 (1972): 149–173.

——, trans. *Tales of Times Now Past: Sixty-two Stories from a Medieval Japanese Collection*. Berkeley: University of California Press, 1979.

Waters, Virginia Skord. "Sex, Lies, and the Illustrated Scroll: The *Dōjōji Engi Emaki*." *Monumenta Nipponica* 52, no. 1 (1997): 59–84.

Yanagita, Kunio. *The Legends of Tōno*. Translated by Ronald A. Morse. Tokyo: Japan Foundation, 1975.

STUDIES

Deal, William E. "Women and Japanese Buddhism." In *Religions of Japan in Practice*, edited by George J. Tanabe Jr., 176–184. Princeton, N.J.: Princeton University Press, 1999.

Eubanks, Charlotte. "Illustrating the Mind: 'Faulty Memory' *Setsuwa* and the Decorative Sutras of Late Classical and Early Medieval Japan." *Japanese Journal of Religious Studies* 36, no. 2 (2009): 209–230.

——. "Rendering the Body Buddhist: Sermonizing in Medieval Japan." Ph.D. diss., University of Colorado at Boulder, 2005.

Foster, Michael Dylan. *Pandemonium and Parade: Japanese Monsters and the Culture of Yōkai*. Berkeley: University of California Press, 2009.

Geddes, Ward. "The Courtly Model: Chōmei and Kiyomori in *Jikkinshō*." *Monumenta Nipponica* 42, no. 2 (1987): 157–166.

Howell, Thomas Raymond, Jr. "*Setsuwa*, Knowledge, and the Culture of Reading and Writing in Medieval Japan." Ph.D. diss., University of Pennsylvania, 2002.

Kelsey, W. Michael. *Konjaku monogatari-shū*. Boston: Twayne, 1982.

——. "*Konjaku monogatari-shū*: Toward an Understanding of Its Literary Qualities." *Monumenta Nipponica* 30, no. 2 (1975): 121–150.

——. "Salvation of the Snake, the Snake of Salvation: Buddhist–Shintō Conflict and Resolution." *Japanese Journal of Religious Studies* 8, nos. 1–2 (1981): 83–113.

Kimbrough, R. Keller. *Preachers, Poets, Women, and the Way: Izumi Shikibu and the Buddhist Literature of Medieval Japan*. Ann Arbor: Center for Japanese Studies, University of Michigan, 2008.

Klein, Susan Blakeley. "When the Moon Strikes the Bell: Desire and Enlightenment in the Noh Play *Dōjōji*." *Journal of Japanese Studies* 17, no. 2 (1991): 291–322.

——. "Woman as Serpent: The Demonic Feminine in the Noh Play *Dōjōji*." In *Religious Reflections on the Human Body*, edited by Jane Marie Law, 100–136. Bloomington: Indiana University Press, 1995.

Kobayashi, Hiroko. *The Human Comedy of Heian Japan: A Study of the Secular Stories in the Twelfth-Century Collection of Tales, Konjaku monogatarishū*. Tokyo: Centre for East Asian Cultural Studies, 1979.

Kotas, Fredric. "Ōjōden: Accounts of Rebirth in the Pure Land." Ph.D. diss., University of Washington, 1987.

LaFleur, William R. *The Karma of Words: Buddhism and the Literary Arts in Medieval Japan*. Berkeley: University of California Press, 1983.

Li, Michelle Osterfeld. *Ambiguous Bodies: Reading the Grotesque in Japanese Setsuwa Tales*. Stanford, Calif.: Stanford University Press, 2009.

Mills, Douglas E. "Popular Elements in Heian Literature." *Journal-Newsletter of the Association of Teachers of Japanese* 3, no. 3 (1966): 38–41.

Mori, Masato. "*Konjaku monogatari-shū*: Supernatural Creatures and Order." Translated by W. Michael Kelsey. *Japanese Journal of Religious Studies* 9, nos. 2–3 (1982): 147–170.

Morrell, Robert E. "Mirror for Women: Mujū Ichien's *Tsuma kagami*." *Monumenta Nipponica* 35, no. 1 (1980): 45–75.

Rodd, Laurel Rasplica. "Nichiren and *Setsuwa*." *Japanese Journal of Religious Studies* 5, nos. 2–3 (1978): 159–185.

Tonomura, Hitomi. "Black Hair and Red Trousers: Gendering the Flesh in Medieval Japan." *American Historical Review* 99, no. 1 (1994): 129–154.

Ury, Marian. "A Heian Note on the Supernatural." *Journal of the Association of Teachers of Japanese* 22, no. 2 (1988): 189–194.

Wilson, William Ritchie. "The Way of the Bow and Arrow: The Japanese Warrior in *Konjaku monogatari*." *Monumenta Nipponica* 28, no. 2 (1973): 177–233.

Major Plays of Chikamatsu, tr. Donald Keene 1961

Four Major Plays of Chikamatsu, tr. Donald Keene. Paperback ed. only. 1961; rev. ed. 1997

Records of the Grand Historian of China, translated from the Shih chi of Ssu-ma Ch'ien, tr. Burton Watson, 2 vols. 1961

Instructions for Practical Living and Other Neo-Confucian Writings by Wang Yang-ming, tr. Wing-tsit Chan 1963

Hsün Tzu: Basic Writings, tr. Burton Watson, paperback ed. only. 1963; rev. ed. 1996

Chuang Tzu: Basic Writings, tr. Burton Watson, paperback ed. only. 1964; rev. ed. 1996

The Mahābhārata, tr. Chakravarthi V. Narasimhan. Also in paperback ed. 1965; rev. ed. 1997

The Manyōshū, Nippon Gakujutsu Shinkōkai edition 1965

Su Tung-p'o: Selections from a Sung Dynasty Poet, tr. Burton Watson. Also in paperback ed. 1965

Bhartrihari: Poems, tr. Barbara Stoler Miller. Also in paperback ed. 1967

Basic Writings of Mo Tzu, Hsün Tzu, and Han Fei Tzu, tr. Burton Watson. Also in separate paperback eds. 1967

The Awakening of Faith, Attributed to Aśvaghosha, tr. Yoshito S. Hakeda. Also in paperback ed. 1967

Reflections on Things at Hand: The Neo-Confucian Anthology, comp. Chu Hsi and Lü Tsu-ch'ien, tr. Wing-tsit Chan 1967

The Platform Sutra of the Sixth Patriarch, tr. Philip B. Yampolsky. Also in paperback ed. 1967

Essays in Idleness: The Tsurezuregusa of Kenkō, tr. Donald Keene. Also in paperback ed. 1967

The Pillow Book of Sei Shōnagon, tr. Ivan Morris, 2 vols. 1967

Two Plays of Ancient India: The Little Clay Cart and the Minister's Seal, tr. J. A. B. van Buitenen 1968

The Complete Works of Chuang Tzu, tr. Burton Watson 1968

The Romance of the Western Chamber (Hsi Hsiang chi), tr. S. I. Hsiung. Also in paperback ed. 1968

The Manyōshū, Nippon Gakujutsu Shinkōkai edition. Paperback ed. only. 1969

Records of the Historian: Chapters from the Shih chi of Ssu-ma Ch'ien, tr. Burton Watson. Paperback ed. only. 1969

Cold Mountain: 100 Poems by the T'ang Poet Han-shan, tr. Burton Watson. Also in paperback ed. 1970

Twenty Plays of the Nō Theatre, ed. Donald Keene. Also in paperback ed. 1970

Chūshingura: The Treasury of Loyal Retainers, tr. Donald Keene. Also in paperback ed. 1971; rev. ed. 1997

The Zen Master Hakuin: Selected Writings, tr. Philip B. Yampolsky 1971

Chinese Rhyme-Prose: Poems in the Fu Form from the Han and Six Dynasties Periods, tr. Burton Watson. Also in paperback ed. 1971

Kūkai: Major Works, tr. Yoshito S. Hakeda. Also in paperback ed. 1972

The Old Man Who Does as He Pleases: Selections from the Poetry and Prose of Lu Yu, tr. Burton Watson 1973

The Lion's Roar of Queen Śrīmālā, tr. Alex and Hideko Wayman 1974

Courtier and Commoner in Ancient China: Selections from the History of the Former Han by Pan Ku, tr. Burton Watson. Also in paperback ed. 1974

Japanese Literature in Chinese, vol. 1: Poetry and Prose in Chinese by Japanese Writers of the Early Period, tr. Burton Watson 1975

Japanese Literature in Chinese, vol. 2: Poetry and Prose in Chinese by Japanese Writers of the Later Period, tr. Burton Watson 1976

Love Song of the Dark Lord: Jayadeva's Gītagovinda, tr. Barbara Stoler Miller. Also in paperback ed. Cloth ed. includes critical text of the Sanskrit. 1977; rev. ed. 1997

Ryōkan: Zen Monk-Poet of Japan, tr. Burton Watson 1977

Calming the Mind and Discerning the Real: From the Lam rim chen mo of Tsoṇ-kha-pa, tr. Alex Wayman 1978

The Hermit and the Love-Thief: Sanskrit Poems of Bhartrihari and Bilhaṇa, tr. Barbara Stoler Miller 1978

The Lute: Kao Ming's P'i-p'a chi, tr. Jean Mulligan. Also in paperback ed. 1980

A Chronicle of Gods and Sovereigns: Jinnō Shōtōki of Kitabatake Chikafusa, tr. H. Paul Varley 1980

Among the Flowers: The Hua-chien chi, tr. Lois Fusek 1982

Grass Hill: Poems and Prose by the Japanese Monk Gensei, tr. Burton Watson 1983

Doctors, Diviners, and Magicians of Ancient China: Biographies of Fang-shih, tr. Kenneth J. DeWoskin. Also in paperback ed. 1983

Theater of Memory: The Plays of Kālidāsa, ed. Barbara Stoler Miller. Also in paperback ed. 1984

The Columbia Book of Chinese Poetry: From Early Times to the Thirteenth Century, ed. and tr. Burton Watson. Also in paperback ed. 1984

Poems of Love and War: From the Eight Anthologies and the Ten Long Poems of Classical Tamil, tr. A. K. Ramanujan. Also in paperback ed. 1985

The Bhagavad Gita: Krishna's Counsel in Time of War, tr. Barbara Stoler Miller 1986

The Columbia Book of Later Chinese Poetry, ed. and tr. Jonathan Chaves. Also in paperback ed. 1986

The Tso Chuan: Selections from China's Oldest Narrative History, tr. Burton Watson 1989

Waiting for the Wind: Thirty-six Poets of Japan's Late Medieval Age, tr. Steven Carter 1989

Selected Writings of Nichiren, ed. Philip B. Yampolsky 1990

Saigyō, Poems of a Mountain Home, tr. Burton Watson 1990

The Book of Lieh Tzu: A Classic of the Tao, tr. A. C. Graham. Morningside ed. 1990

The Tale of an Anklet: An Epic of South India—The Cilappatikāram of Iḷaṅkō Aṭikaḷ, tr. R. Parthasarathy 1993

Waiting for the Dawn: A Plan for the Prince, tr. with introduction by Wm. Theodore de Bary 1993

Yoshitsune and the Thousand Cherry Trees: A Masterpiece of the Eighteenth-Century Japanese Puppet Theater, tr., annotated, and with introduction by Stanleigh H. Jones, Jr. 1993

The Lotus Sutra, tr. Burton Watson. Also in paperback ed. 1993

The Classic of Changes: A New Translation of the I Ching *as Interpreted by Wang Bi*, tr. Richard John Lynn 1994

Beyond Spring: Tz'u Poems of the Sung Dynasty, tr. Julie Landau 1994

The Columbia Anthology of Traditional Chinese Literature, ed. Victor H. Mair 1994

Scenes for Mandarins: The Elite Theater of the Ming, tr. Cyril Birch 1995

Letters of Nichiren, ed. Philip B. Yampolsky; tr. Burton Watson et al. 1996

Unforgotten Dreams: Poems by the Zen Monk Shōtetsu, tr. Steven D. Carter 1997

The Vimalakirti Sutra, tr. Burton Watson 1997

Japanese and Chinese Poems to Sing: The Wakan rōei shū, tr. J. Thomas Rimer and Jonathan Chaves 1997

Breeze Through Bamboo: Kanshi of Ema Saikō, tr. Hiroaki Sato 1998

A Tower for the Summer Heat, by Li Yu, tr. Patrick Hanan 1998

Traditional Japanese Theater: An Anthology of Plays, by Karen Brazell 1998

The Original Analects: Sayings of Confucius and His Successors (0479–0249), by E. Bruce Brooks and A. Taeko Brooks 1998

The Classic of the Way and Virtue: A New Translation of the Tao-te ching *of Laozi as Interpreted by Wang Bi*, tr. Richard John Lynn 1999

The Four Hundred Songs of War and Wisdom: An Anthology of Poems from Classical Tamil, The Puṟanāṉūṟu, ed. and tr. George L. Hart and Hank Heifetz 1999

Original Tao: Inward Training (Nei-yeh) *and the Foundations of Taoist Mysticism*, by Harold D. Roth 1999

Lao Tzu's Tao Te Ching: *A Translation of the Startling New Documents Found at Guodian*, by Robert G. Henricks 2000

The Shorter Columbia Anthology of Traditional Chinese Literature, ed. Victor H. Mair 2000

Mistress and Maid (Jiaohongji), by Meng Chengshun, tr. Cyril Birch 2001

Chikamatsu: Five Late Plays, tr. and ed. C. Andrew Gerstle 2001

The Essential Lotus: Selections from the Lotus Sutra, tr. Burton Watson 2002

Early Modern Japanese Literature: An Anthology, 1600–1900, ed. Haruo Shirane 2002; abridged 2008

The Columbia Anthology of Traditional Korean Poetry, ed. Peter H. Lee 2002

The Sound of the Kiss, or The Story That Must Never Be Told: Pingali Suranna's Kalapurnoday-amu, tr. Vecheru Narayana Rao and David Shulman 2003

The Selected Poems of Du Fu, tr. Burton Watson 2003

Far Beyond the Field: Haiku by Japanese Women, tr. Makoto Ueda 2003

Just Living: Poems and Prose by the Japanese Monk Tonna, ed. and tr. Steven D. Carter 2003

Han Feizi: Basic Writings, tr. Burton Watson 2003

Mozi: Basic Writings, tr. Burton Watson 2003

Xunzi: Basic Writings, tr. Burton Watson 2003

Zhuangzi: Basic Writings, tr. Burton Watson 2003

The Awakening of Faith, Attributed to Aśvaghosha, tr. Yoshito S. Hakeda, introduction by Ryuichi Abe 2005

The Tales of the Heike, tr. Burton Watson, ed. Haruo Shirane 2006

Tales of Moonlight and Rain, by Ueda Akinari, tr. with introduction by Anthony H. Chambers 2007

Traditional Japanese Literature: An Anthology, Beginnings to 1600, ed. Haruo Shirane 2007

The Philosophy of Qi, by Kaibara Ekken, tr. Mary Evelyn Tucker 2007

The Analects of Confucius, tr. Burton Watson 2007

The Art of War: Sun Zi's Military Methods, tr. Victor Mair 2007

One Hundred Poets: One Poem Each: A Translation of the Ogura Hyakunin Isshu, tr. Peter McMillan 2008

Zeami: Performance Notes, tr. Tom Hare 2008

Zongmi on Chan, tr. Jeffrey Lyle Broughton 2009

Scripture of the Lotus Blossom of the Fine Dharma, rev. ed., tr. Leon Hurvitz, preface and introduction by Stephen R. Teiser 2009

Mencius, tr. Irene Bloom, ed. with an introduction by Philip J. Ivanhoe 2009

Clouds Thick, Whereabouts Unknown: Poems by Zen Monks of China, Charles Egan 2010

The Mozi: A Complete Translation, tr. Ian Johnston 2010

The Huainanzi: A Guide to the Theory and Practice of Government in Early Han China, by Liu An, tr. John S. Major, Sarah A. Queen, Andrew Seth Meyer, and Harold D. Roth, with Michael Puett and Judson Murray 2010